CB126694

American Inside Out Evolution

Student's Book | Beginner

SUE KAY
VAUGHAN JONES

macmillan education

Contents

	Units and topics	Speaking and Writing	Reading and Listening	Grammar, Vocabulary, and Pronunciation
Page 8	0 Instructions **Classroom**	Activities to introduce classroom language including teacher and textbook instructions		
Page 10	1 ID **Names and numbers** **Everyday objects**	S Exchanging names and numbers S Identifying everyday objects WB W Punctuation (question mark/period) Writing short questions and answers	L James Bond L What's in your bag? **Language for Life:** Personal Information **Life Skills** Studying: Materials	G *my/ your/ his/ her.* Singular and plural nouns. *this/ these* V Names. Numbers 1-10. Everyday Objects. P Alphabet. Vowel Sounds
Page 16	2 International **Countries** **Nationalities** **Prices**	S Saying where you are from S Talking about prices	L Rock star talent L Prices around the world **Language for Life:** In a store **Life Skills** Cultural Awareness: Food and Celebrations	G *be*: simple present Prepositions: *in/near How much ...?* V Countries. Nationalities. Numbers 11-199. Prices P Word stress: numbers
Page 22	3 Family **Family** **Introductions**	S Talking about your family W Someone in your family	L My family (1) L My family (2) R Famous families **Language for Life:** Introductions **Life Skills** Communication: Showing Interest	G *How old ...?* Possessive *'s/s'. our/ their. have/ has.* V Family P *an* + vowel / *a* + consonant
Page 28	Review A	Pages 28, 29: **Grammar / Vocabulary / Pronunciation review** Pages 30, 31: **Reading & Listening, Writing (form filling) & Speaking**		

	Units and topics	Speaking and Writing	Reading and Listening	Grammar, Vocabulary, and Pronunciation
Page 32	4 Life **Lifestyle** **Daily routine** **Work**	S Talking about your lifestyle S Talking about a dream job S Telling the time WB W Building a description of a daily routine from notes	L What's your dream job? R DJ Luiz **Language for Life:** Time **Life Skills** Time Management: My Day	G Simple present: *I, he, she, it, you, we, they.* The time. V Jobs. Daily routines. Days. P 3rd person verb endings
Page 38	5 Places **Location** **City Attractions**	S Talking about NYC S Talking about places to go W A city WB W Linking sentences (*and* and *but*); description (city)	L People in NYC R The top 5 things to do in NYC **Language for Life:** Asking about location **Life Skills** Decision Making: Where to Live	G *there is/there are. some/any* V Places in a city. Verb phrases with *go* P Weak forms in *There's a ...* and *There are ...*
Page 44	6 Clothes **Clothes** **Shopping**	S Talking about clothes S Talking about current activities WB W Posting on instagram	L The catwalk L Three conversations R Clothes around the world **Language for Life:** In a clothing store **Life Skills** Organization: *How often do you ...?*	G Present progressive. *How often ...?* Adverbs of frequency. V Colors. Clothes. Verb phrases P *ing* forms
Page 50	Review B	Pages 50, 51: **Grammar / Vocabulary / Pronunciation review** Pages 52, 53: **Reading & Listening, Writing (personal profile) & Speaking**		

Pairwork	page 54
Grammar Extra	page 58
Audio Script	page 62

Walkthrough

VOCABULARY

- Vocabulary is presented in a meaningful context and is related to the topics in the unit.
- Clear pictures help acquisition.
- There are practice activities to expand your knowledge of particular lexical sets and give you opportunities to use the new vocabulary in social exchanges.
- You will also listen to the words and repeat them before manipulating them in real social contexts.

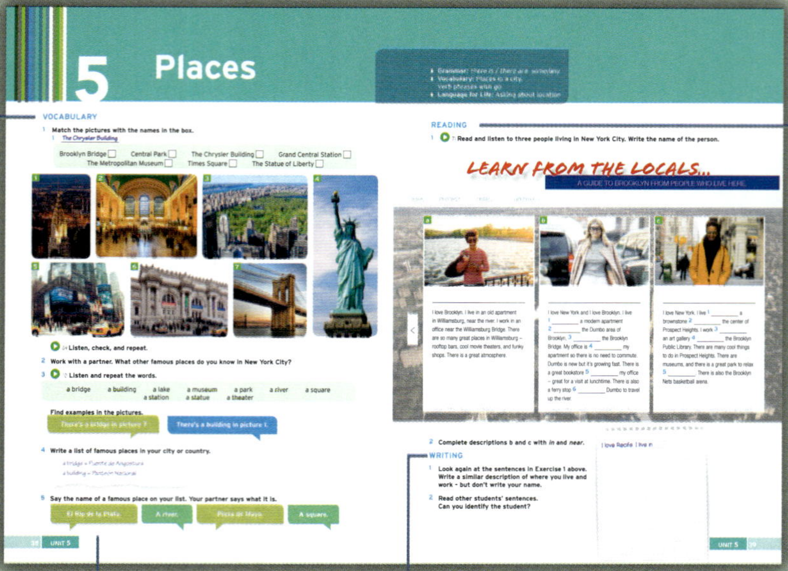

READING

Contemporary reading texts have been adapted and graded to suit each level They have been selected not only for their language content but also for their interest and appropriacy. The texts are supported by recordings.

SPEAKING

You will have plenty of opportunities to speak throughout the unit using language learned.

WRITING

Motivating writing practice is provided in a task where you will follow a model. The writing activities are also based on varied texts that you will write on everyday life. There is also a comprehensive writing course in the Workbook.

PRONUNCIATION

Pronunciation work on particular areas of sound, stress, and intonation is integrated into every unit.

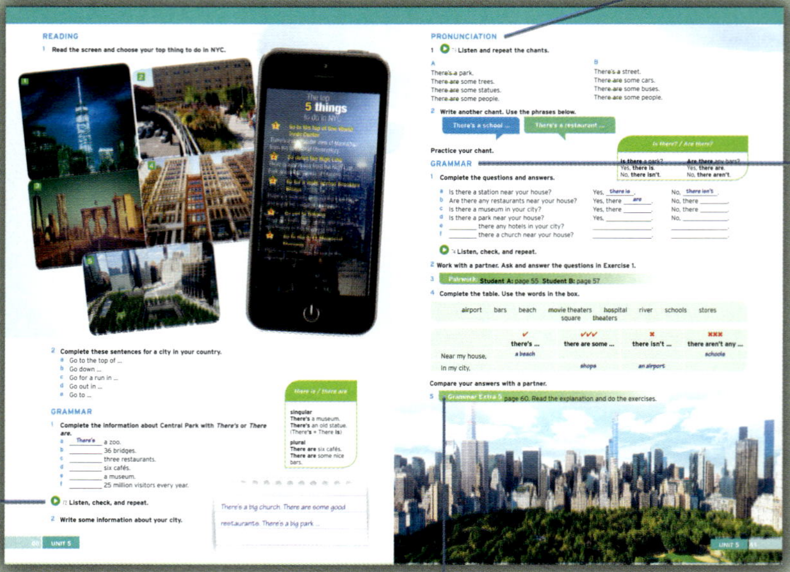

GRAMMAR

- Here you will explore new grammatical structures that have been contextualized in the reading / listening sections. You will focus on the way language works.
- A brief summary of the grammar point is provided in the margin.
- Language is explored in realistic and meaningful practice exercises.
- You will use target language in controlled and personalized practice.

LISTENING

The listening activities include texts specially written for language learning – dialogues, conversations and monologues. They were carefully designed to develop real life listening skills.

- The Grammar Extra pages at the back of the Student's Book extend explanations and provide further practice.

LANGUAGE FOR LIFE

The Language for Life section gives you a portable toolkit of functional language. Here, you notice how language is more than just form. You will see language in fun, engaging social situations. The section is recorded on the audio CD too.

VOCABULARY EXTRA

The Vocabulary Extra pages at the end of every unit recycle the key vocabulary items taught in the unit. This provides an activated wordlist and a useful bank of vocabulary.

LIFE SKILLS

Developing life skills alongside language skills is an essential requirement to meet the demands of the contemporary world.

American Inside Out Evolution has a Life Skills section in every unit. Life Skills present activities in order for you to reflect on and discuss the skills you need for social and work situations in today's world.

REVIEW

There are Review units in the Student's Book. Each Review unit reviews the new structures and vocabulary taught in the previous teaching units.

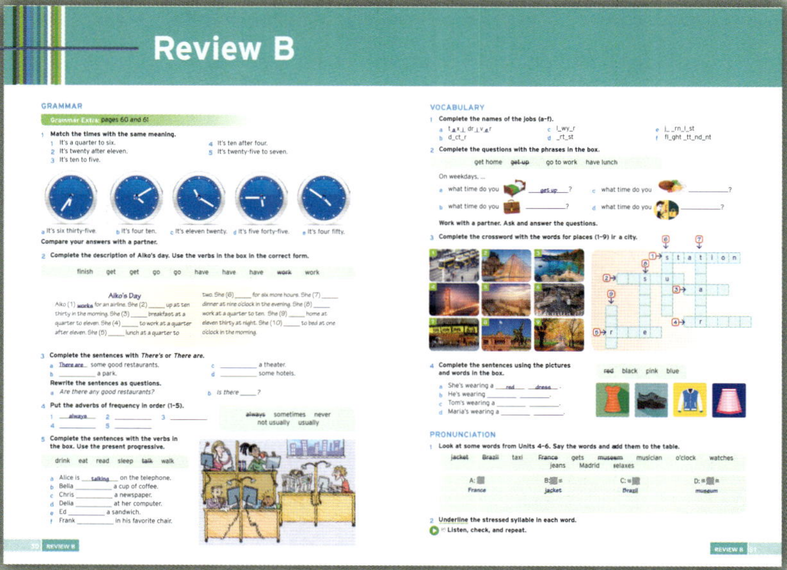

There is one Pairwork activity for every unit, which offers further speaking practice.

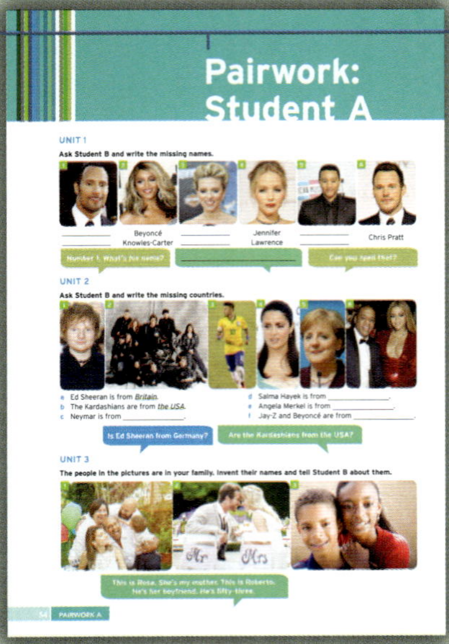

Pairwork: Student A

UNIT 1

UNIT 2

UNIT 3

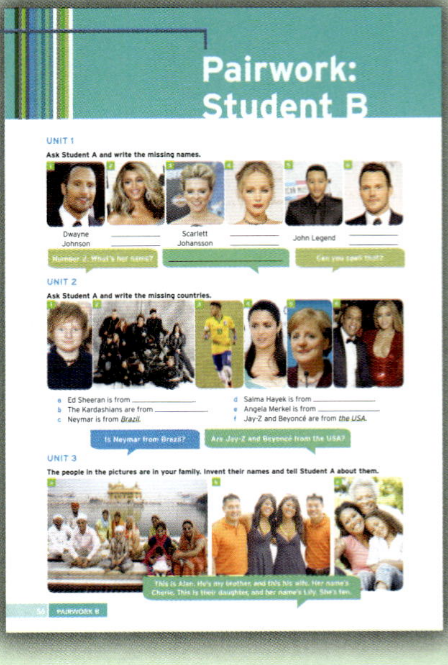

Pairwork: Student B

UNIT 1

UNIT 2

UNIT 3

GRAMMAR EXTRA

The Grammar Extra pages at the back of the Student's Book provide a summary of the new grammatical structures, as well as extra practice.

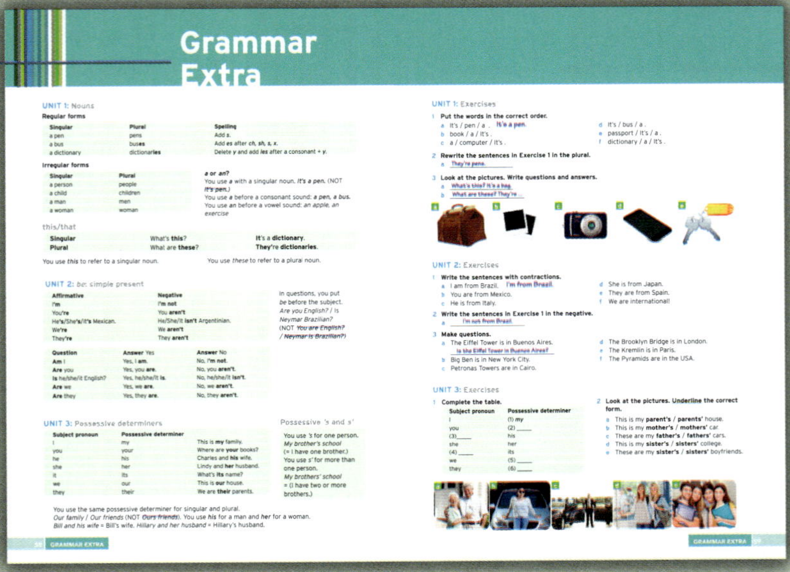

Grammar Extra

UNIT 1: Nouns

UNIT 2: *be*: simple present

UNIT 3: Possessive determiners

UNIT 1: Exercises

UNIT 2: Exercises

UNIT 3: Exercises

The Workbook provides a review of all the main points in the Student's Book, plus extra listening practice, pronunciation work, and a writing program.

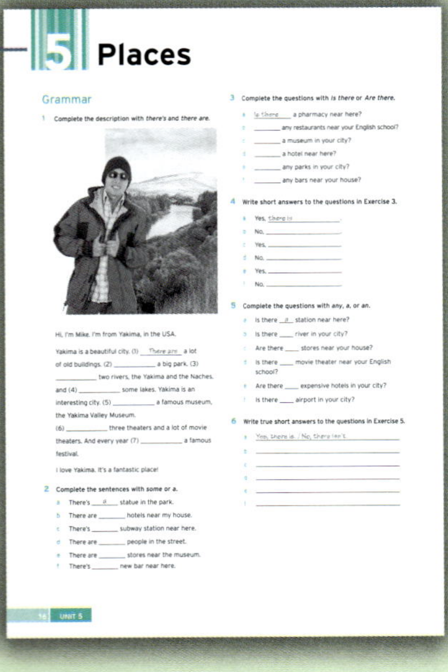

5 Places

Grammar

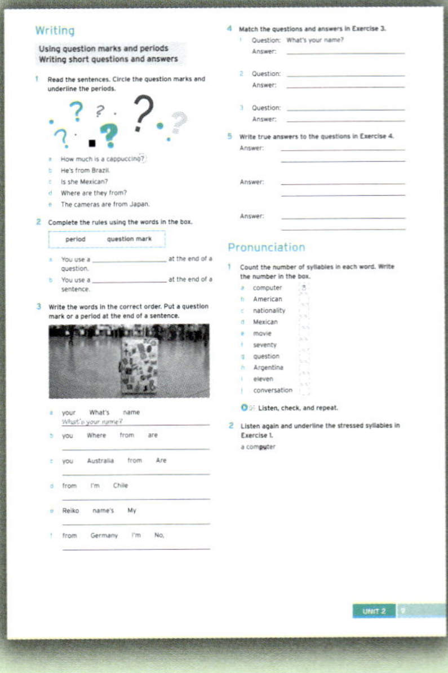

Writing

Pronunciation

Student's Components

Student's Book with access code to Digital Student's Book

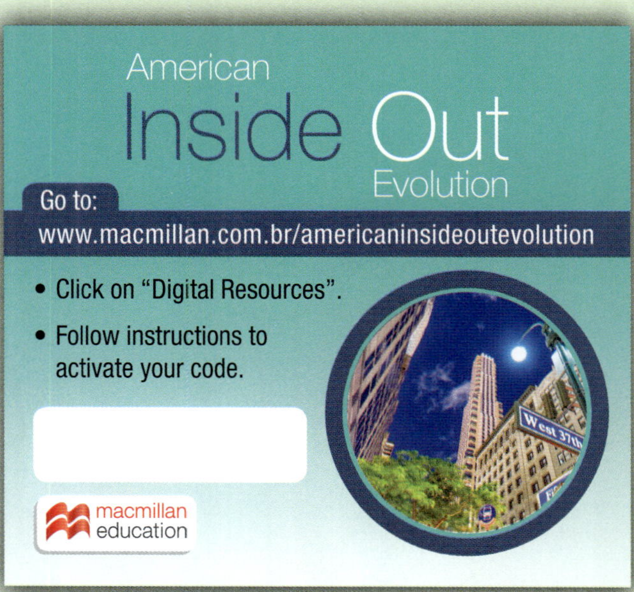

Workbook with access code to Digital Workbook

0 Instructions

1 ▶ 2 **Listen and repeat the instructions.**

Ask. Answer. Listen. Speak.

Point. Look. Write. Read.

2 ▶ 3 **Listen and repeat the instructions.**

a

Look at the pictures.

b

Listen and repeat.

c

Practice the conversation.

d

Read the text.

e

Compare your answers.

f

Check your answers.

3 ▶ 4 **Read and listen to the instructions.**

- a **Complete.** Hello. My name's _Mario_.
- b **Circle.** Hello. My name's Mario.
- c **Underline.** Hello. My name's Mario.
- d **Check. (✔)** 1☐ 2☐ 3☑ 4☐
- e **Cross out.** Hello. My name's ~~Mario~~.
- f **Match.**
  1 France
  2 Brazil
  3 Japan

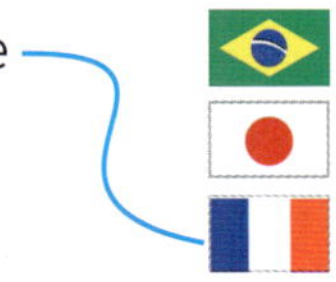

4 Follow the instructions.

- a **Complete the sentence.** Hello. My name's ____________.
- b **Circle the name.** Hello. My name's Tina.
- c **Underline *Hello*.** Hello. My name's Luis.
- d **Check (✔) the correct box.** I'm a man (♂). ☐ I'm a woman (♀) ☐
- e **~~Cross out~~ the incorrect word.** Inglish English
- f **Match the numbers.**
  1 two
  2 three
  3 one

1 ID

GRAMMAR

1 **Read the dialogue.**

Possessive determiners

my name
your name

***be:* contractions**

I'**m** = I **am**
My name'**s** = My name **is**
What'**s** = What **is**

- What's your name?
- My name's Bond ... James Bond.

2 **Complete the dialogue with *my* or *your*.**

- Hello. I'm Madeleine Swann. What's _______ name?
- _______ name's Bond ... James Bond.
- Nice to meet you, James.

Practice the dialogue with a partner.

SPEAKING

1 5 **Listen and complete.**

- Hello. _______ Sandra. What's _______ name?
- Hello, Sandra. _______ name's Diego. Nice to meet _______.

2 **Speak to other students. Practice the dialogue with your names.**

Hello, I'm Manolo. What's your name?

My name's Ana Ramirez.

Nice to meet you, Ana.

- **Grammar:** *my/your/his/her.* Singular and plural nouns. *this/these*
- **Vocabulary:** Names. Numbers 1-10. Everyday objects
- **Language for Life:** Personal information

GRAMMAR

1 6 **Listen and complete with *his* or *her*.**

a What's ______ name? ______ name's Daniel Craig.
b What's ______ name? ______ name's Naomi Harris.

2 **Ask questions about students in your class.**

What's his name? — Rafael.
What's her name? — Maria.

Possessive determiners

her name **his** name

VOCABULARY

1 7 **Listen and repeat the numbers.**

Numbers

0 = zero / oh
1 = one
2 = two
3 = three
4 = four
5 = five
6 = six
7 = seven
8 = eight
9 = nine
10 = ten
007 = double oh, seven

2 **Complete the lists.**

a one two three ______ ______
b five four ______ ______ ______
c two four ______ ______ ______
d one three five ______ ______

8 **Listen, check, and repeat.**

3 9 **Listen and write the telephone numbers.**

a What's your cell phone number?
302 ____ ____
b What's your home number?
____ ____ ____

SPEAKING

1 **Ask two students. Complete the information.**

What's your first name? — Dimitri.
What's your last name? — Fernandes.

1 FIRST NAME ______
LAST NAME ______
HOME ______
CELL PHONE ______

2 FIRST NAME ______
LAST NAME ______
HOME ______
CELL PHONE ______

Names

first name = James
last name = Bond

VOCABULARY

1 ▶ 10 **Listen and repeat the words.**

1 a bag
2 a computer
3 books
4 pens
5 keys
6 a cell phone
7 a passport
8 a camera

2 **Cover the words. Say a number. Your partner says the word.**

Two. | A computer. | Four. | Pens.

GRAMMAR

1 **Look at the picture above. Underline the correct answer.**

a	What's this?	**It's a bag. / They're bags.**
b	What's this?	**It's a computer. / They're computers.**
c	What are these?	**It's a book. / They're books.**
d	What are these?	**It's a pen. / They're pens.**
e	What are these?	**It's a key. / They're keys.**
f	What's this?	**It's a cell phone. / They're cell phones.**
g	What's this?	**It's a passport. / They're passports.**
h	What's this?	**It's a camera. / They're cameras.**

▶ 11 **Listen, check, and repeat.**

Nouns; *this/these*

Singular
What's **this**?
It's a pen.

Plural
What are **these**?
They're **pens**.

It'**s** = It **is**
They'**re** = They **are**

2 **Grammar Extra 1** page 58. Read the explanation and do the exercises.

LISTENING

1 ▶ 12 **Listen to the conversation. Check (✓) the things in her bag. Check (✓) the things in his bag.**

Her bag	Things	His bag
✓	a computer	______
______	a camera	______
______	books	______
______	a cell phone	______
______	a passport	______

2 **What *isn't* in his bag?**

PRONUNCIATION

1 ▶ 13 **Listen and repeat the letters.**

2 ▶ 14 **Listen and complete with the letters in the box.**

A E I O U

1 /i/ B C D E G P T V Z
2 /e/ F L M N S X
3 /eɪ/ _ H J K
4 /u/ Q _ W
5 /aɪ/ _ Y
6 /ou/ _
7 /a/ R

The alphabet

A B	C D	E F	G
H I	J K	L M N O	P
Q R	S	T U	V
W	X	Y	Z

3 ▶ 15 **Listen and number (1–6).**

______ OK
______ CIA
______ VIP
______ CNN
______ UK
______ USA

Listen, check, and repeat.

LANGUAGE FOR LIFE

1 ▶ 16 **Read, listen, and complete the conversation.**

Receptionist: Welcome to The Oxford English School. What's your name?
Student: Yolanda.
Receptionist: Can you spell that, please?
Student: Y-O-L-A-N-D-A.
Receptionist: And your last name?
Student: **(1)** C-A-S-_____________.
Receptionist: Sorry, can you repeat that, please?
Student: **(2)** _____________.
Receptionist: Thank you, Ms. **(3)** _____________.
Student: Please call me Yolanda.
Receptionist: OK. Thank you, Yolanda.

Listen and check.

2 ▶ 17 **Listen and repeat the expressions.**
a Can you spell that, please?
b Sorry, can you repeat that, please?
c Please call me Yolanda.

3 **Work with a partner. Write a new conversation about one of these students.**

Practice the conversation.

THE OXFORD ENGLISH SCHOOL

FIRST NAME: **Isabella (Bella)**
LAST NAME: **Campanella**

THE OXFORD ENGLISH SCHOOL

FIRST NAME: **Angel**
LAST NAME: **Estevez**

4 **Pairwork: Student A:** page 54 **Student B:** page 56

Life Skills: Studying
Materials

1 **Look at the pictures. Write three items you need to study English.**

My items
1
2
3
4

2 **What other items do you need? Add 1 new item.**
3 **Talk to your partner about your choices.**

A computer, a pen, a ...

MACMILLAN LIFE SKILLS

1 Vocabulary Extra

Everyday Objects

1 **Match the pictures with the words.**

_______ a bag
_______ a book
_______ a camera
_______ a cell phone
_______ a computer
_______ a dictionary
_______ a key
_______ a passport
_______ a pen

2 **Work with a partner. Cover the words. Look at the pictures. Ask and answer questions.**

Numbers

1 **Match the numbers (1-10) with the words in the box.**

eight	five	four	nine	one	seven	six	ten	three	two

1 ___one___
2 __________
3 __________
4 __________
5 __________
6 __________
7 __________
8 __________
9 __________
10 __________

2 **Dictate three numbers to your partner.**

4 6 10

Check your partner's numbers.

four
six
ten

2 International

VOCABULARY

1 18 **Listen to the introductions in *Rock Star Talent* and complete the table.**

Brazil Germany ~~Mexico~~ Japan Chile Spain

●••		●•		•●	●
1 Mexico	2 ______	3 ______	4 ______	5 ______	6 ______

2 19 **Listen and repeat the countries.**
What's the name of your country in English?

GRAMMAR

1 **Complete the answers with *I*, *you*, *he*, *she*, *we*, or *they*.**

a Is Monika from Germany? Yes, she is. No, she isn't.
b Is Rosa from Japan? Yes, ______ is. No, ______ isn't.
c Is Victor from Chile? Yes, ______ is. No, ______ isn't.
d Are Andreas and Ana from Brazil? Yes, ______ are. No, ______ aren't.
e Are you from Spain? Yes, ______ am. No, ______'m not.
f Are you and your teacher from Mexico? Yes, ______ are. No, ______ aren't.

20 **Listen, check, and repeat.**

2 **Work with a partner. Ask and answer the questions in Exercise 1.**

3 **Pairwork: Student A:** page 54 **Student B:** page 56

4 **Grammar Extra 2** page 58. Read the explanation and do the exercises.

be

I**'m** = I **am**
You**'re** = You **are**
He**'s** = He **is**
She**'s** = She **is**
It**'s** = It **is**
We**'re** = We **are**
They**'re** = They **are**
Is Victor from Chile?
Yes, he **is**.
No, he **isn't**.
(is**n't** = is **not**)

- **Grammar:** *be:* simple present. Prepositions: *in/near. How much ...?*
- **Vocabulary:** Countries. Nationalities. Numbers 11-199. Prices
- **Language for Life:** In a store

GRAMMAR

Prepositions

in

near

1 21 **Listen and underline the correct answers.**

a Where are you from?
I'm from Paterna. It's **in** / **near** Valencia **in** / **near** Spain.

b Where are you from?
We're from Niteroi. It's **in** / **near** Rio **in** / **near** Brazil.

Practice the questions and answers.

2 **Complete the sentence.**

I'm from __________. It's (near __________) in __________.

SPEAKING

1 **Ask three students.**

Where are you from?

I'm from Puebla. It's near Mexico City in Mexico.

2 **Ask questions about students in your class.**

Where is Pedro from?

He's from Recife.

Is Gloria from São Paulo?

No, she isn't. She's from Porto Alegre.

VOCABULARY [1]

1 ▶ 22 **Listen and repeat the nationalities.**

2 **Look at the pictures. Underline the correct description.**

a 

b 

c 

d 

e 

f 

a She's **Brazilian** / **British**.
b It's **Mexican** / **Spanish**.
c He's **Spanish** / **American**.
d They're **Chilean** / **Brazilian**.
e They're **German** / **British**.
f They're **Mexican** / **Japanese**.

▶ 23 **Listen, check, and repeat.**

Nationalities

American 

Brazilian 

British 

Chilean 

German 

Japanese 

Mexican 

Spanish 

VOCABULARY [2]

1 ▶ 24 **Listen and repeat the numbers.**

2 **Say the numbers with a partner.**

3 **Complete each line.**

a 21 = twenty-one   22 = twenty-two   23 = twenty-three
b 34 = thirty-four   35 = thirty-five   36 = ____________
c 47 = forty-seven   48 = forty-eight   49 = ____________
d 111 = one hundred and eleven
112 = one hundred and twelve
113 = ______________________________

▶ 25 **Listen and check.**

4 ▶ 26 **Listen and connect the numbers.**

a	13	30	74
	59	66	81
	98	14	40
b	15	24	119
	50	83	190
	99	199	7
c	18	17	29
	70	80	38
	79	116	160

What's the mystery number?

Numbers

11 = eleven
12 = twelve
13 = thirteen
14 = fourteen
15 = fifteen
16 = sixteen
17 = seventeen
18 = eighteen
19 = nineteen
20 = twenty
30 = thirty
40 = forty
50 = fifty
60 = sixty
70 = seventy
80 = eighty
90 = ninety
100 = one hundred

PRONUNCIATION

1 **Match the words with the signs.**

a	euros	R$
b	pounds	$
c	dollars	€
d	real	£

27 **Listen and repeat the words.**

2 28 **Listen and circle the price you hear.**

a	($3.50)	$3.15	e	€18.20	€80.20
b	£5.30	£5.13	f	£40.40	£14.40
c	€17.75	€70.75	g	$160.00	$116.00
d	R$90.99	R$19.99			

Listen again and repeat the prices.

LISTENING

1 29 **Listen and complete the table with the missing prices.**

	a cappuccino	a hamburger	a movie ticket	a night in a 3-star hotel
1 NEW YORK	a $5.00	$8.00	$14.00	$170.00
2 MEXICO CITY	$4.50	b ______	$10.00	$90.00
3 ROME	$2.50	$6.00	$12.85	$140.00
4 LONDON	$3.00	$7.60	c ______	$190.00
5 TOKYO	$4.20	$5.50	$18.45	d ______
6 ______	______	______	______	______

(prices in US dollars)

Work with a partner. Complete row 6 in the table with the prices in your city.

GRAMMAR

1 **Put the words in the correct order.**

a in New York? / is / a cappuccino / How much
How much is a cappuccino in New York?

b How much / in London? / a hamburger / is

c is / a movie ticket / How much / in Tokyo?

d a night in a 3-star hotel / in Mexico City? / is / How much

30 **Listen, check, and repeat the questions.**

2 **Work with a partner. Ask and answer the questions in Exercise 1.**

How much ...?

How much is a cappuccino in New York?

Three dollars.

LANGUAGE FOR LIFE

1 Complete the conversation with the words in the box.

are · is · these · ~~this~~

a

How much is this ?
Twenty dollars fifty.
OK, thanks.

b

How much are ______?
Nine dollars.
OK, thanks.

c

How much ______ this?
Eight euros twenty.
OK, thanks.

d

How much ______ these?
One hundred and seventy-five dollars.
Oh! OK, no thanks.

31 **Listen and check.**

2 32 **Listen and repeat the expressions.**

3 Work with a partner. Practice the conversations.

Life Skills: Cultural Awareness
Food and Celebrations

1 Look at the pictures. Write using the words in the box.

American · Spanish · ~~British~~ · Japanese · German · Mexican

a British b ______ c ______ d ______ e ______ f ______

33 **Listen, check, and repeat.**

2 Write the country.

a It's the Rio Carnival. Brazil
b It's the Thanksgiving Day parade. ______
c It's Oktoberfest. ______
d It's the Day of the Dead. ______

34 **Listen, check, and repeat.**

3 Play a guessing game.

Hamburger. Where am I from?

The USA.

Carnival. Where am I from?

Brazil!

MACMILLAN LIFE SKILLS

2 Vocabulary Extra

Countries and Nationalities

1 Look at the pictures. For each picture write:

a the country
b the nationality

Use the words in the box.

American Spain Chilean ~~Mexico~~ Japanese Brazil Japan German
the UK the USA Brazilian Germany ~~Mexican~~ Chile British Spanish

1

Mexico City

a Mexico
b Mexican

2

Berlin

a ____________
b ____________

3

Madrid

a ____________
b ____________

4

New York

a ____________
b ____________

5

Santiago

a ____________
b ____________

6

Kyoto

a ____________
b ____________

7

Rio de Janeiro

a ____________
b ____________

8

London

a ____________
b ____________

Numbers

1 Match the numbers with the words in the box.

11	*eleven*	17	________	50	________
12	________	18	________	60	________
13	________	19	________	70	________
14	________	20	________	80	________
15	________	30	________	90	________
16	________	40	________	100	________

eighteen eighty ~~eleven~~ fifteen
fifty forty fourteen nineteen
ninety one hundred seventeen
seventy sixteen sixty thirteen
thirty twelve twenty

2 Dictate the numbers to your partner.

19 50 100

nineteen
fifty
one hundred

Check your partner's numbers.

3 Family

LISTENING

1 35 **Listen to Luisa and match the family words with the names.**

1 father (dad)	Ana
2 mother (mom)	Victor
3 brother	Lucas
4 sister	Maria
5 grandmother (grandma)	Julia
6 grandfather (grandpa)	Bruno

2 36 **Listen and repeat the family words.**

3 **Complete the family tree.**

Key
= married to
♂ male
♀ female

Luisa's Family

♂ a) Victor (70) = ♀ b) ________ (68)

♂ c) ________ (42) = ♀ d) Julia (42)

♂ e) ________ (4) ♀ f) Luisa (6) ♀ g) ________ (1)

GRAMMAR

1 37 **Listen and complete the questions and answers.**

a How old are you? I'm six.
b How old is your brother? He's four.
c How old ________ your sister? ________ one.
d How old ________ your mother and father? ________ forty-two.
e How old ________ your grandmother? ________ sixty-eight.
f How old ________ your grandfather? ________ seventy.

How old ...?

How old are you?
I'm 24.

2 **Work with a partner. Ask and answer the questions in Exercise 1.**

- **Grammar:** *How old ...?* Possessive *'s/s'*. *our/their. have/has*
- **Vocabulary:** Family
- **Language for Life:** Introductions

GRAMMAR

Possessive *'s / s'*

My brother**'s** name is Bruno.
(brother**'s** is singular)

My sister**s'** names are Luisa and Ana.
(sister**s'** is plural)

1 **Complete the sentences.**

a Julia is Luisa's *mother*.
b Bruno is Luisa's ________.
c Victor is Luisa's ________.
d Ana is Luisa's ________.
e Lucas is Luisa's ________.
f Maria is Luisa's ________.

▶ 38 **Listen, check, and repeat.**

2 **Match the descriptions (a-c) with the names *Ana*, *Julia*, and *Bruno*.**

a His father's name is Lucas, and his sisters' names are Luisa and Ana. Who is he? ________
b Her brother's name is Bruno, and her sister's name is Luisa. Who is she? ________
c Her father's name is Victor, and her mother's name is Maria. Who is she? ________

LISTENING

1 ▶ 39 **Listen to Victor. Put the family pictures (a-c) in the correct order (1-3).**

a

Julia and Lucas

b

Victor and Maria

c

Luisa and Ana

2 **Listen again. Underline the correct word.**

a Maria is Victor's **husband** / **wife**.
b Julia is Victor's **son** / **daughter**.
c Ana is Victor's **grandson** / **granddaughter**.

VOCABULARY

1 ▶ 40 **Listen and repeat the family words.**

Family						
♀	mother	daughter	grandmother	granddaughter	sister	wife
♂	father	son	grandfather	grandson	brother	husband
♀♂	parents	children	grandparents	grandchildren		

2 **Write six more sentences about Victor and Luisa's family.**

1 Victor is Maria's husband.
2 Lucas and Julia are Luisa's parents.

3 **Who are you? Write six sentences.**

1 I'm Mindy's son.
2 I'm Natasha's brother.
3 I'm Dimitri's grandson.

Compare with a partner.

4 **Pairwork: Student A:** page 54 **Student B:** page 56

READING

1 41 **Read the texts.**

NEWS SHOWS MOVIES COMPETITIONS

a

Hello to the Smiths!

Who's on the red carpet? It's the Smith family! *Fresh Prince of Bel Air* actor and movie star, Will Smith is married to actor Jada Pinkett-Smith. They have two children. And their children are stars now! Jaden Smith is an actor and singer, and he was in the movies *Karate Kid* and *After Earth*. Jaden has a little sister, Willow. She is young, but she has a hit song already, with *Whip My Hair*. Will's oldest son, Trey, from his first marriage, is a DJ in Los Angeles.

b

It's A Cyrus Family Event!

That is the Cyrus family at the music awards. Father, Billy Ray Cyrus, a famous singer, enjoyed the evening with his wife, Leticia. Billy and Leticia have three children. Miley Cyrus is a big TV and music star, and her sister, Noah, is also a pop singer.

2 **Who says it? Match the sentences (a-d) with the correct names (1-4).**

a My mother is an actor. My brother is Jaden.
b I'm a singer. My children are singers and their names are Miley and Noah.
c I'm an actor. My wife is also an actor. We have two children.
d Our dad is a famous singer. Our mom is called Leticia.

1 Miley and Noah Cyrus ☐
2 Billy Ray Cyrus ☐
3 Will Smith ☐
4 Willow Smith ☐

GRAMMAR

1 **Complete the sentences with *my*, *his*, *her*, *our*, or *their*.**

a Jada Pinkett-Smith and __her__ daughter are actors.
b Billy Ray Cyrus and ______ daughters are singers.
c Jaden, Willow, and ______ parents are all famous stars.
d Miley Cyrus says, "______ sister and I are now singers. ______ parents are so proud!"
e Noah Cyrus is happy to be a singer like ______ sister and ______ father.

42 **Listen, check and repeat.**

Possessive determiners

I → **my** mother
you → **your** father
he → **his** sister
she → **her** brother
we → **our** children
they → **their** parents

2 **Grammar Extra 3:** page 58. Read the explanation and do the exercises.

GRAMMAR

1 **Underline the correct form.**

a I **has** / **have** one brother.
b My parents **has** / **have** a dog.
c My mother **has** / **have** three brothers.
d My grandparents **has** / **have** two houses.
e My husband and I **has** / **have** two children.
f My father **has** / **have** a Japanese car.

43 **Listen, check, and repeat.**

2 **Which sentences are true for you?**

have

I **have**
You **have**
He **has**
She **has**
It **has**
We **have**
They **have**

PRONUNCIATION

1 44 **Listen and repeat.**

a He's a teacher. She's an actor.
b He has a Samsung Galaxy. She has an iPhone.
c He has a Japanese car. She has an American car.

2 **Complete the table with the nouns in the box.**

~~Oreo cookie~~ ~~brother~~ dog English dictionary Android cell phone Gucci bag Apple computer American grandmother passport sister

an **+ vowel sound**	***a*** **+ consonant sound**
an Oreo cookie	*a brother*

45 **Listen, check, and repeat.**

3 **Tell your partner about things you have. Use *a* or *an*.**

I have a dog.

I have an English textbook.

WRITING

1 **Write about someone in your family. See the example.**

Lourdes is my grandmother. She's my mother's mother. She's seventy-three. She's from Villa Vicencio near Bogotá in Colombia. She has four children and seven grandchildren. Her husband's name is Juan.

2 **Compare with a partner.**

LANGUAGE FOR LIFE

1 ▶ 46 **Read and listen to the conversations. Answer the questions.**

a Who's Anna's brother?
b Who's Becky's husband?

Tim: This is Anna. She's my sister.
Gerry: Nice to meet you. I'm Gerry.
Anna: Nice to meet you.

Rob: This is Sophia. She's Brazilian.
Becky: Nice to meet you. I'm Rob's wife.
Sophia: Nice to meet you.

2 ▶ 47 **Listen and repeat the expressions.**

3 **Complete the conversation with the words in the box.**

'm meet Nice ~~This~~ to you

Anna: **1** This is Tim.
Sophia: **2** ________ to **3** ________ you. I **4** ________ Sophia.
Tim: Nice **5** ________ meet **6** ________.

▶ 48 **Listen and check.**

4 **Work in groups of three. Rewrite the conversation with your names. Practice the conversation.**

Life Skills: Communication
Showing Interest

see Really right way

1 ▶ 49 **Listen and complete the conversations using the words in the box.**

a **Anna:** Who's this?
Bridget: This is my grandmother, Anna. She's ninety-three.
Anna: ________?
Bridget: Yes. She looks amazing, doesn't she?

c **Shen:** Who's this in the photo?
Jenny: He's my grandfather, Ben. He's seventy-two. He runs marathons.
Shen: No ________!
Jenny: I know. We all think he's crazy ...

b **Luis:** And who's this?
Fran: Oh, this is my sister, Esther. She's a doctor at the city hospital.
Luis: Is that ________?
Fran: Yes. She's very smart!

d **Pippa:** And who's the boy?
Tom: Ah, that's my son, Will.
Pippa: Where is he?
Tom: He's at his grandparents.
Pippa: Oh, I ________.

2 **We can use these expressions to show interest. Are they normal responses or strong responses? Write N or S.**

a I see. N
b That's amazing. ____
c That's interesting. ____
d No way! ____
e Really? ____
f Right. ____
g You're kidding! ____

▶ 50 **Listen, check, and repeat.**

3 **Practice with a partner.**

This is my grandfather. He's eighty.

Really?

MACMILLAN LIFE SKILLS

3 Vocabulary Extra

Family

1 **Complete the sentences with the words in the box.**

brother	granddaughter	grandfather
husband	mother	parents

1

Alice is Bill's wife.

Bill is Alice's ___husband___.

2

Karl is Alice and Bill's son.

Alice and Bill are Karl's __________.

3

Alice is Linda's grandmother.

Linda is Alice's __________.

4

Linda is Ed's sister.

Ed is Linda's __________.

5

Ed is Fran's son.

Fran is Ed's __________.

6

Gary is Karl's grandson.

Karl is Gary's __________.

2 **Look at the family tree and answer the questions.**

a Who is Linda's father?
b Who is Fran's daughter?
c Who is Karl's wife?
d Who is Fran's grandson?
e Who are Ed's grandparents?
f Who is Gary's grandmother?

3 **Write sentences about your family.**

Maria is my wife. Rosa is my …

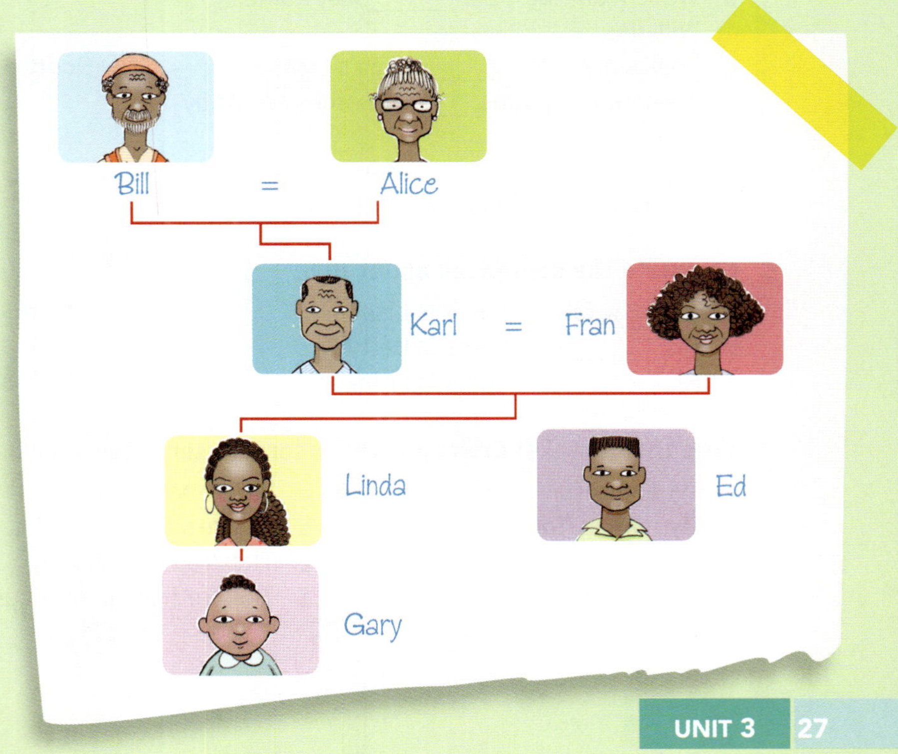

Review A

GRAMMAR

Grammar Extra: pages 58 and 59

1 **Put the words in the correct order.**

a your / What's / name / mother's ?
What's your mother's name?
b is / How / she / old ?
c is / Where / she / from ?
d her / What's / nationality ?
e number / What's / telephone / her ?
f is / Where / now / she ?

Answer the questions. Write sentences.

a *My mother's name is Ana.*

2 **Write questions and answers.**

a *What's this? It's a car.*
b *What are these? ...*

3 **Choose a word in the box to describe each object in Exercise 2.**

American English German Japanese Mexican

a *It's German.*

4 **Look at the family tree. Complete the sentences with *my*, *your*, *his*, *her*, *our*, or *their*.**

a My name's Bob. This is __my__ family.
b We're from the USA. _______ last name's Williams.
c This is my wife. _______ name's Lisa.
d These are my sons. _______ names are Andy and David.
e This is my father. _______ name's Frank.
f You're an English student. What's _______ name?

Frank = Betty
Scott Alec Karen Bob = Lisa
Andy David

5 **Complete the sentences about Bob.**

a His __wife's__ name is Lisa.
b His __________ name is Betty.
c His __________ name is Frank.
d His __________ names are Andy and David.
e His __________ name is Karen.
f His __________ names are Scott and Alec.

6 **Find the mistake! Cross out the incorrect sentence, a or b.**

1 a ~~My name Tom~~.
b My name's Tom.
2 a What is?
b What's this?
3 a Where Mario from?
b Where's Mario from?
4 a They're from Mexico.
b They're from in Mexico.
5 a I'm twenty.
b I have twenty years.
6 a She has two children.
b She have two children.

VOCABULARY

1 **Complete the instructions with the verbs in the box.**

Ask ~~Listen~~ Look Match Practice

a ___Listen___ and repeat.
b ________ the conversation.
c ________ your partner.
d ________ at the pictures.
e ________ the pictures with the words.

2 **Complete the crossword with the numbers one to ten.**

3 **Complete the sentences.**

a Santiago is the capital of ___Chile___.
b Tokyo is the capital of ________.
c Madrid is the capital of ________.
d Mexico City is the capital of ________.
e Brasilia is the capital of ________.

4 **Write the prices.**

a $12.55 ___Twelve dollars and fifty-five cents___
b £24.99 ________
c €15.75 ________
d R$37.80 ________

5 **Complete the pairs.**

a son and ___daughter___
b father and ________
c husband and ________
d brother and ________
e daughter and ________
f mother and ________
g wife and ________
h grandfather and ________
i sister and ________
j granddaughter and ________

PRONUNCIATION

1 **Look at some words from Units 1-3. Say the words and add them to the table.**

~~adjective~~ ~~computer~~ description Mexico granddaughter ~~Japanese~~ possessive Chilean seventeen singular

A: ■■■	B: ■■■	C: ■■■
adjective	com**pu**ter	Japa**nese**

2 Underline the stressed syllable in each word.

51 **Listen, check, and repeat.**

READING & LISTENING

1 Read the information about the West Side Hotel. Are the sentences true or false?

a The West Side Hotel is in San Jose. ________
b It's near the park. ________
c It has a hundred and forty rooms. ________
d A room for one night is $190. ________
e The hotel has a seafood restaurant. ________

West Side Hotel | Check-in | Check-out | **Search**

Luxury in the heart of San Francisco.

Hotel information:

- near the park, galleries, and nightlife
- 120 rooms
- price: $190 per night
- seafood restaurant, breakfast buffet

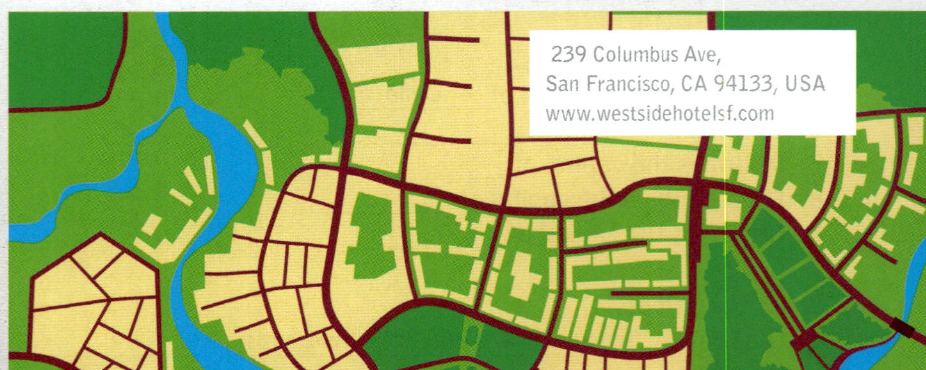

2 52 **Listen to the conversation. Underline the correct information.**

a The woman books: 1 one night 2 two nights 3 three nights
b She's: 1 German 2 Mexican 3 Chilean
c Her room number: 1 44 2 88 3 48

3 Listen again and complete the information on the form.

West Side Hotel — Customer Details

FIRST NAME:	P _ _ l _
LAST NAME:	E _ _ i _ _ z _
NATIONALITY:	_ _ _ _ _ _ _
CITY:	Mexico City
COUNTRY:	Mexico
TELEPHONE NUMBER:	5 5 _ 1 _ 0 5 _ _ 2
PASSPORT NUMBER:	G 4 8 9 - _ _ _ - 2 3

WRITING & SPEAKING

1 Complete the rules for capital letters. Use examples from the West Side Hotel form below.

You use capital letters for ...

a first names: Susan

b last names: ______

c nationalities: ______

d street names: ______

e cities: ______

f countries: ______

West Side Hotel — Customer Details

FIRST NAME:	Susan
LAST NAME:	Barclay
NATIONALITY:	British
ADDRESS:	14, Wellington Street
CITY:	London
COUNTRY:	United Kingdom
TELEPHONE NUMBER:	020-8676-644
EMAIL ADDRESS:	susanb@bmail.co.uk
PASSPORT NUMBER:	761211501
DATE:	06/30
SIGNATURE:	*Susan Barclay*

2 Match the questions (a-g) with the information (1-7) in the form below.

a What's your nationality? ☐

b What's your last name? ☐

c What's your telephone number? ☐

d What's your address? ☐

e What's your email address? ☐

f What's your first name? ☐

g What's your passport number? ☐

West Side Hotel — Customer Details

1 FIRST NAME: ______

2 LAST NAME: ______

3 NATIONALITY: ______

4 ADDRESS: ______

CITY: ______

COUNTRY: ______

5 TELEPHONE NUMBER: ______

6 EMAIL ADDRESS: ______

7 PASSPORT NUMBER: ______

DATE: ______

SIGNATURE: ______

Ask your partner the questions. Complete the form with their information.

4 Life

READING

1 **Read and complete the questionnaire.**

How to score

1: a 2 b 4	**5:** a 1 b 2	**30 to 42:** Your life expectancy is 100.
2: a 2 b 4	**6:** a 6 b 2	**20 to 29:** Your life expectancy is 75.
3: a 6 b 2	**7:** a 4 b 2	**10 to 19:** Change your life!
4: a 8 b 2	**8:** a 0 b 8	

Your life expectancy

Check a or b.

1	You are:	a male ♂ ☐	b female ♀ ☐		2	You live in a big city (3 million people +):	a Yes ☐	b No ☐	
3	You have old people in your family (75+):	a Yes ☐	b No ☐		4	You like your job:	a Yes ☐	b No ☐	
5	You work:	a inside ☐	b outside ☐		6	You eat healthy food:	a Yes ☐	b No ☐	
7	You sleep 6-8 hours:	a Yes ☐	b No ☐		8	You smoke:	a Yes ☐	b No ☐	

2 **Compare your score and your answers with a partner.**

VOCABULARY

1 **Complete the sentences with *eat, have, like, live, speak,* or *work*.**

a I __live__ in an old house. / with my parents.
b I ________ one brother. / an old car.
c I ________ in an office. / for Apple.
d I ________ swimming.
e I ________ English. / Japanese.
f I ________ meat. / vegetables.

53 **Listen, check, and repeat.**

2 **Write six sentences about you. Use the verbs in Exercise 1.**

I live in a big apartment.
I have three children.
I work ...

GRAMMAR

1 **Complete the answers.**

a Do you speak Chinese? Yes, I __do__. No, I __don't__.
b Do you smoke? Yes, I do. No, I ______.
c Do you and your family live in a city? Yes, we do. No, we ______.
d Do your friends like soccer? Yes, they do. No, they ______.
e Do you eat meat? Yes, ______. No, ______.
f Do your parents have a dog? Yes, ______. No, ______.

54 **Listen, check, and repeat.**

Simple present: *I, you, we, they*

I / You / We / They **speak** English.
I / You / We / They **don't speak** Spanish.

Do you **speak** Chinese?
Yes, I **do**.
No, I **don't**.

2 **Put the words in the correct order.**

a live / you / Where / do ? *Where do you live?*
b Where / you / do / work ?
c languages / you / speak / What / do ?
d like / What / food / you / do ?
e you / music / What / like / do ?
f sports / do / What / like / you ?

55 **Listen, check, and repeat.**

3 **Work with a partner. Ask and answer the questions in Exercise 2.**

- **Grammar:** Simple present: *I, he, she, it, you, we, they*. The time.
- **Vocabulary:** Jobs. Daily routines. Days.
- **Language for Life:** Greetings

VOCABULARY

1 **Match the sentences about jobs with the pictures (a-f).**

She's a pilot. ☐ He's a musician. ☐ He's a soccer player. ☐ He's a taxi driver. ☐
She's an artist. ☐ He's a lawyer. ☐

a 
b 
c 
d 
e 
f 

56 **Listen, check, and repeat.**

2 57 **Listen and repeat more sentences about jobs.**

a I'm a flight attendant. ☐

b I'm a doctor. ☐

c I'm a personal assistant. ☐

d I'm a farmer. ☐

e I'm a sales clerk. ☐

f I'm a journalist. ☐

3 **Pairwork: Student A:** page 55 **Student B:** page 57

LISTENING

1 58 **Listen to interviews with five people (1-5). Put the number of each person next to their real job and their dream job.**

Real job		Dream job	
☐ taxi driver	[1] teacher	☐ doctor	☐ soccer player
☐ actor	☐ student	☐ DJ	☐ actor
☐ lawyer		☐ pilot	[1] musician

2 **Ask three people in the class questions.**

What do you do?

I'm a teacher.

What's your dream job?

Model.

VOCABULARY

1 59 **Listen and repeat the days of the week.**

2 **Ask and answer the questions.**

Do you work on Monday?

Yes, I do.

Do you work on Sunday?

No, I don't.

Days	
Sunday	Monday
Tuesday	Wednesday
Thursday	Friday
Saturday	

VOCABULARY

1 60 **Listen and repeat the verb phrases.**

a

get up

b

go to bed

c

have breakfast

d

have lunch

e

have dinner

f

go to work

g

finish work

h

get home

2 **Look at the verb phrases in 1. Number them in the order they happen (1-8).**

READING

1 **Read about DJ Luiz. Answer the questions.**

- a Where does he work?
- b What's the name of his favorite club?

Superstar DJ!

DJLuiz

follow

Sky Studios

567 likes 2d

Hey, fans! Happy Wednesday! This is my routine during the week. I **1** ________ up early, have breakfast, and take my son to school. Then I **2** ________ to the gym – have to stay fit and healthy. After that I **3** ________ to work in a recording studio. Right now, we're in Sky Studios. It's a beautiful place. After I finish work, I **4** ________ home and **5** ________ dinner with my family. We have two young children, River and Lake, so we all **6** ________ to bed early. Nice!

Add a comment ...

Club Liquid

248 likes 1d

Hey, guys! Another Saturday night – who wants to have some fun? On Saturdays, I **7** ________ to bed in the afternoon and then I go to work. I work all night in the club. I love DJing all night! My favorite club is Club Liquid in São Paulo, but I work in clubs all around the world. Visit my website www.djluiz.com for club dates. I work hard, but I also **8** ________ a good time. So, who's ready for a BIG night?

Add a comment ...

2 **Complete the text with *get*, *go*, or *have*.**

61 **Listen and check.**

3 **Look at these sentences about DJ Luiz. Are they true or false?**

- a On weekdays, he gets up early.
- b On weekdays, he takes his son to school.
- c On weekdays, he goes to bed in the afternoon.
- d On Saturdays, he finishes work and goes to the studio.
- e On Saturdays, he works all night.

GRAMMAR

1 **Complete the questions and answers about DJ Luiz.**

a Does he go to the gym on weekdays? Yes, he *does*. No, he *doesn't*.
b Does he have children? Yes, he _______. No, he _______.
c Does he go to bed in the evening on Saturdays? Yes, he _______. No, he _______.
d _______ he work in clubs all around the world? _______. _______.
e _______ he like his job? _______. _______.

62 **Listen, check, and repeat.**

Simple present: *he, she, it*

He **works** all night.
He **doesn't work** at home.
(doesn**'t** = does **not**)
Does she **like** dance music?
Yes, she **does**.
No, she **doesn't**.

2 **Work with a partner. Ask and answer the questions in Exercise 1.**

3 **Grammar Extra 4** page 60. Read the explanation and do the exercises.

PRONUNCIATION

1 63 **Listen and repeat the verbs.**

A		B	
Same number of syllables with *he/she/it*		**Extra syllable with *he/she/it***	
do	does	finish	finishes
get	gets	relax	relaxes
go	goes	teach	teaches
have	has	watch	watches

LISTENING

1 64 **Listen and complete the times.**

a San Francisco *4:00 a.m.*
b Buenos Aires ____________
c London ____________
d Moscow ____________
e Hong Kong ____________
f Wellington ____________

GRAMMAR

1 **Complete the table.** ***What time is it?***

a	4:00 a.m.	→	It's four o'clock in the morning.
b	8:00 a.m.	→	____________ in the morning.
c	________	→	It's noon.
d	3:00 p.m.	→	____________ in the afternoon.
e	8:00 p.m.	→	____________ in the evening.
f	________	→	It's midnight.

65 **Listen, check, and repeat.**

The time

What time is it?
It's three o'clock.

It's six thirty.
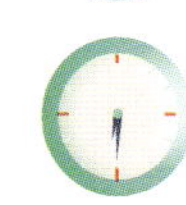

It's a quarter after twelve.

It's a quarter to twelve.

2

a It's two twenty-five.
It's twenty-five after two.

b *It's seven fifty.*
It's ten to eight.

c It's three ____________.
It's twenty-five to four.

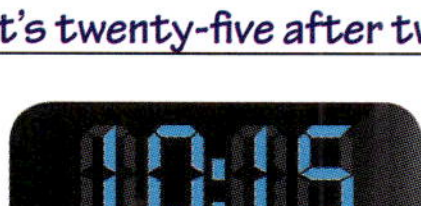

d It's ten ____________.
It's a ____________.

e ____________-oh-five.
It's five ____________.

f It's twelve ____________.
It's a ____________.

66 **Listen, check, and repeat.**

LANGUAGE FOR LIFE

1 67 **Read and listen to the conversations. Answer the questions.**

a What time is it in New York?

b What time is it in Sydney?

Mr. Edwards: Hello.
John: Good morning! Is this Mr. Edwards?
Mr. Edwards: Who is this?
John: It's John from New York.
Mr. Edwards: What time is it in New York, John?
John: It's 8:30 in the morning.
Mr. Edwards: Oh. Do you know what time it is in Sydney, John?
John: Er, no. What time is it in Sydney, Mr. Edwards?
Mr. Edwards: It's 11:30 ... p.m.
John: Oh, good evening, Mr. Edwards.
Mr. Edwards: Goodnight, John.

Practice the conversation.

2 68 **Listen and repeat the expressions.**

3 **Work with a partner. Complete a similar telephone conversation between Ms. Harper in Los Angeles and her personal assistant, Jenny, in London.**

Ms. Harper: Hello.
Jenny: Good afternoon! Is this Ms. Harper?
Ms. Harper: Who is this?
Jenny: Jenny ...

Practice the conversation.

Life Skills: Time Management

My Day

1 **Create a schedule for a typical day.**
2 **Do you have any free time? Discuss with a partner.**
3 **Re-write your schedule including more time for English study.**

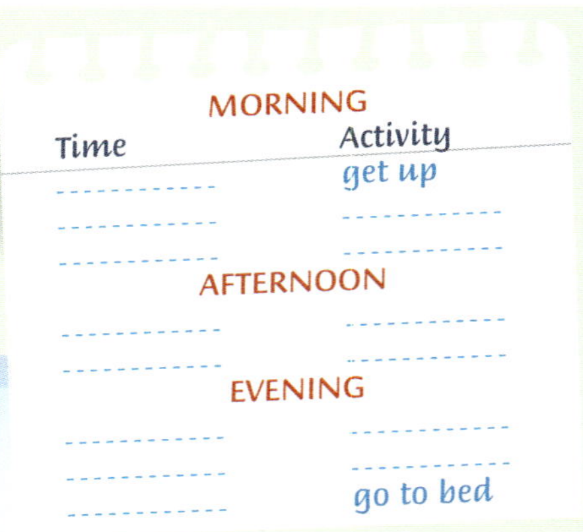

MACMILLAN LIFE SKILLS

4 Vocabulary Extra

Jobs

1 Match the pictures with the words.

_____ a doctor
_____ a sales clerk
_____ a flight attendant
_____ an actor
_____ a soccer player
_____ a DJ
_____ a pilot
_____ a farmer
_____ a secretary
_____ a journalist
_____ a lawyer
_____ a musician
_____ an artist
_____ a taxi driver
_____ a teacher

2 Work with a partner. Cover the words. Look at the pictures. Ask and answer questions.

What does he do?

He's a farmer.

The day

1 Match the pictures with the words.

_____ morning
_____ afternoon
_____ midnight
_____ noon
_____ evening
_____ night

2 When do you do these things?

get up	morning
go to bed	_____
finish work	_____
have breakfast	_____
have lunch	_____
watch TV	_____

5 Places

VOCABULARY

1 Match the pictures with the names in the box.

Brooklyn Bridge ☐ Central Park ☐ The Chrysler Building 1 Grand Central Station ☐
The Metropolitan Museum ☐ Times Square ☐ The Statue of Liberty ☐

1

2

3

4

5

6

7

69 **Listen, check, and repeat.**

2 Work with a partner. What other famous places do you know in New York City?

3 70 **Listen and repeat the words.**

a bridge a building a lake a museum a park a river a square
a station a statue a theater

Find examples in the pictures.

There's a bridge in picture 7.

There's a building in picture 1.

4 Write a list of famous places in your city or country.

a bridge = Puente de Angostura
a building = Panteón Nacional

5 Say the name of a famous place on your list. Your partner says what it is.

El Rio de la Plata.

A river.

Plaza de Mayo.

A square.

- **Grammar:** *there is/there are. Some/any*
- **Vocabulary:** Places in a city.
  Verb phrases with *go*
- **Language for Life:** Asking about location

READING

1 71 **Read and listen to three people living in New York City. Write the name of the person.**

LEARN FROM THE LOCALS...

A GUIDE TO BROOKLYN FROM PEOPLE WHO LIVE HERE.

HOME FEATURES TRAVEL LIFESTYLE

a

____

I love Brooklyn. I live in an old apartment in Williamsburg, near the river. I work in an office near the Williamsburg Bridge. There are so many great places in Williamsburg – rooftop bars, cool movie theaters, and funky shops. There is a great atmosphere.

reply like follow November 17 at 12.41pm

b

____

I love New York and I love Brooklyn. I live **1** _________ a modern apartment **2** _________ the Dumbo area of Brooklyn, **3** _________ the Brooklyn Bridge. My office is **4** _________ my apartment so there is no need to commute. Dumbo is new but it's growing fast. There is a great bookstore **5** _________ my office – great for a visit at lunchtime. There is also a ferry stop **6** _________ Dumbo to travel up the river.

reply like follow November 17 at 2.45pm

c

____

I love New York. I live **1** _________ a brownstone **2** _________ the center of Prospect Heights. I work **3** _________ an art gallery **4** _________ the Brooklyn Public Library. There are many cool things to do in Prospect Heights. There are museums, and there is a great park to relax **5** _________. There is also the Brooklyn Nets basketball arena.

reply like follow November 17 at 5.13pm

2 **Complete descriptions b and c with *in* and *near*.**

WRITING

1 **Look again at the sentences in Exercise 1 above. Write a similar description of where you live and work – but don't write your name.**

2 **Read other students' sentences. Can you identify the student?**

I love Recife. I live in ...

READING

1 **Read the screen and choose your top thing to do in NYC.**

1

2

3

4

5

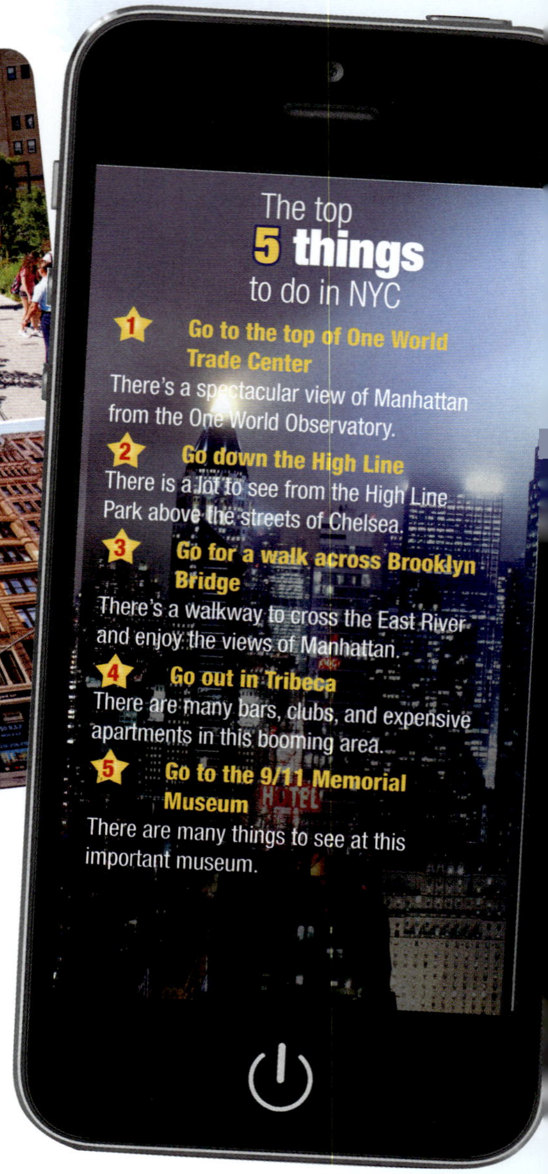

2 **Complete these sentences for a city in your country.**

- a Go to the top of ...
- b Go down ...
- c Go for a run in ...
- d Go out in ...
- e Go to ...

GRAMMAR

1 **Complete the information about Central Park with *There's* or *There are.***

- a ___There's___ a zoo.
- b __________ 36 bridges.
- c __________ three restaurants.
- d __________ six cafés.
- e __________ a museum.
- f __________ 25 million visitors every year.

72 **Listen, check, and repeat.**

2 **Write some information about your city.**

there is/there are

singular
There's a museum.
There's an old statue.
(There**'s** = There **is**)

plural
There are six cafés.
There are some nice bars.

There's a big church. There are some good restaurants. There's a big park ...

PRONUNCIATION

1 73 **Listen and repeat the chants.**

A
There's a park.
There are some trees.
There are some statues.
There are some people.

B
There's a street.
There are some cars.
There are some buses.
There are some people.

2 **Write another chant. Use the phrases below.**

There's a school ... There's a restaurant ...

Practice your chant.

GRAMMAR

Is there?/Are there?

Is there a park?	**Are there** any bars?
Yes, **there is**.	Yes, **there are**.
No, **there isn't**.	No, **there aren't**.

1 **Complete the questions and answers.**

a	Is there a station near your house?	Yes, there is.	No, there isn't.
b	Are there any restaurants near your house?	Yes, there are.	No, there ______.
c	Is there a museum in your city?	Yes, there ______.	No, there ______.
d	Is there a park near your house?	Yes, ______.	No, ______.
e	______ there any hotels in your city?	______.	______.
f	______ there a church near your house?	______.	______.

74 **Listen, check, and repeat.**

2 **Work with a partner. Ask and answer the questions in Exercise 1.**

3 **Pairwork: Student A:** page 55 **Student B:** page 57

4 **Complete the table. Use the words in the box.**

airport bars beach movie theaters hospital river schools stores square theaters

	✔ there's ...	✔✔✔ there are some ...	✖ there isn't ...	✖✖✖ there aren't any ...
Near my house,	a beach			schools
In my city,		shops	an airport	

Compare your answers with a partner.

5 **Grammar Extra 5** page 60. Read the explanation and do the exercises.

LANGUAGE FOR LIFE

1 **Write the names of the places in the box under the correct pictures.**

an ATM	a pharmacy
a restroom	a subway station

a a pharmacy ____________

b ____________

c ____________

d ____________

75 **Listen, check, and repeat.**

2 76 **Read and listen to two tourists in New York. What do they ask for?**

Man: Excuse me. Is 1 ________ a pharmacy 2 ________ here?
Woman: A what?
Man: A pharmacy.
Woman: A 3 ________? Er, yes – over there.
Man: Thanks.

Woman: 4 ________ me. Is 5 ________ a restroom 6 ________ here?
Man: A restroom?
Woman: Yes, yes, a restroom
Man: A restroom? 7 ________ here? No.
Woman: Oh!

3 **Complete the two conversations in Exercise 2. Listen and check.**

4 77 **Listen and repeat the expressions.**
a Excuse me.
b Is there a pharmacy near here?
c Yes – over there.

Life Skills: Decision-making
Where to Live?

1 **Read the post.**

2 **Read about three neighborhoods in New York City.**

> We love New York and we really want to move there. Are there any good places to live in the city? We have two children and we want to live somewhere trendy ...
> @annamarie22 reply · like · follow April 30 at 14.10pm

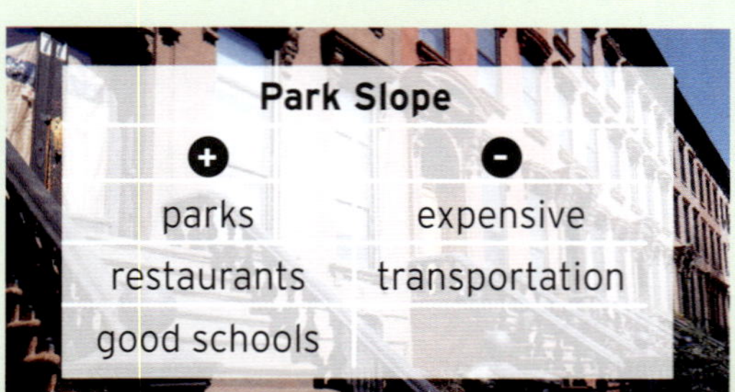

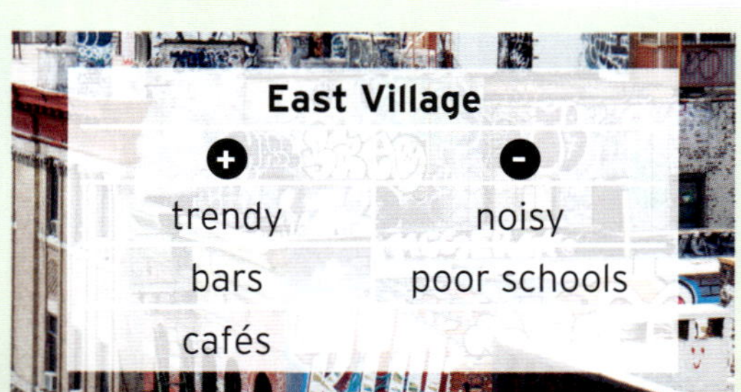

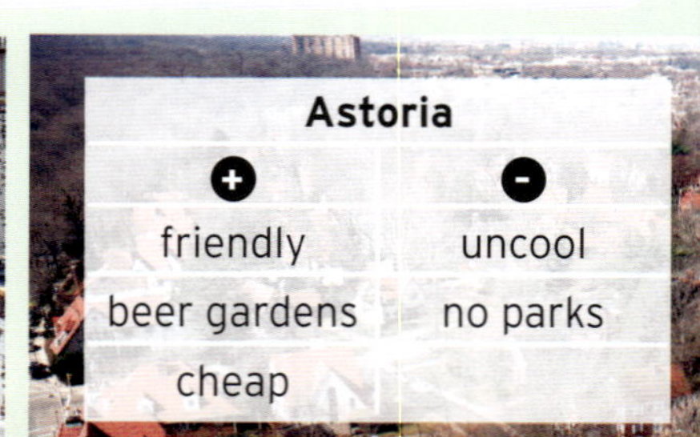

3 **Discuss with your partner and choose the best neighborhood for @annamarie22.**

4 **Write a reply to @annamarie22. Use the words from Exercise 2.**

> Why don't you try ____________? It's ____________.
> There are ____________. There ____________.

MACMILLAN LIFE SKILLS

5 Vocabulary Extra

Town and Country

1 Match the places in the pictures with the words.

14	an airport	______	a lake	______	a school
______	a bar	______	a movie theater	______	a square
______	a beach	______	a museum	______	a station
______	a bridge	______	a park	______	a statue
______	a church	______	a restaurant	______	a theater

2 Work with a partner. Cover the words. Look at the places in the picture. Ask and answer questions.

What's this?

It's a lake.

6 Clothes

VOCABULARY

1 78 **Listen and repeat the colors.**

2 **Say a number. Your partner says which color.**

1 2 3 4 5 6 7 8 9 10

Five

Green

3 **Ask your partner "math" questions.**

What's black, blue, and red?

Eight. (1 + 4 + 3 = 8)

LISTENING & VOCABULARY

1 **Complete the descriptions with the colors.**

a
1 a __black__ jacket
2 a ________ T-shirt
3 ________ pants
4 ________ shoes

c
1 a ________ dress
2 ________ shoes

b
1 a ________ hat
2 a ________ top
3 a ________ skirt
4 ________ boots

d
1 a ________ suit
2 a ________ tie
3 a ________ shirt
4 ________ and
________ sneakers

79 **Listen, check, and repeat.**

2 80 **Listen and match the names with the pictures (a-d).**

Jasmine Kate Jason Leon

- **Grammar:** Present progressive. *How often ...?* Adverbs of frequency.
- **Vocabulary:** Colors. Clothes. Verb phrases.
- **Language for Life:** In a clothing store.

READING

1 ▶ 81 **Read the texts.**

1

It's GRADUATION Day!

As a student, Kumiko usually wears a T-shirt and jeans, but today is a special day for Kumiko and her friends. Kumiko is graduating from college, so she's wearing a hakama. This is traditional Japanese clothing that students wear for graduation day.

2

Fun in Mumbai!

Veena and Sita are having fun this weekend in Mumbai, India. It's their friend's wedding, so they are dressing up. Look at those beautiful Indian clothes! They work in a call center. There Venna and Sita usually wear white shirts and black skirts, but today they are dancing at a wedding in beautiful and colorful silk saris.

3

Off to the races!

Peter and Stan are Physical Education teachers. They usually wear tracksuits, but not today! They're going horse racing. Peter and Stan are wearing hats, suit jackets, striped pants, and waistcoats.

2 **Complete the table with information from the texts.**

	Job	Clothes they usually wear	Clothes in the picture
Veena and Sita	*call center workers*		
Kumiko		*a T-shirt and jeans*	
Peter and Stan			*hats, suit jackets, and waistcoats*

GRAMMAR

1 **Complete the questions and answers about the pictures above.**

a *Are* Veena and Sita wearing black skirts? *Yes, they are.* *No, they aren't.*
b *Are* they dancing? Yes, ________. No, ________.
c Is Peter wearing sneakers? Yes, *he is*. No, *he isn't*.
d ________ Veena and Sita having a great time? ________. ________.
e ________ Kumiko wearing jeans? ________. ________.
f ________ she holding a parasol? ________. ________.

▶ 82 **Listen, check, and repeat.**

Present progressive

I**'m working**.
You**'re working**.
He**'s working**.
She**'s working**.
It**'s working**.
We**'re working**.
They**'re working**.

Are you **working**?
Yes, I **am**.
No, I**'m not**.

2 **Work with a partner. Ask and answer the questions in Exercise 1.**

3 **Pairwork: Student A:** page 55 **Student B:** page 57

4 **Grammar Extra 6** page 60. Read the explanation and do the exercises.

PRONUNCIATION

1 83 **Listen and repeat the chants.**

A
Teaching or learning?
Studying or working?
What are you doing?
What are you doing?

B
Eating or drinking?
Sleeping or thinking?
What are you doing?
What are you doing?

C
Running or walking?
Listening and talking?
What are you doing?
What are you doing?

2 **Write another chant. Use the verbs in the box.**

buy / sell come / go give / take read / write sit / stand stop / start

Practice your chant.

LISTENING

1 **Match the pictures (a-c) with the descriptions (1-3).**

1 A boy is playing a computer game. His mother is calling him from her office.
2 A woman is trying on clothes. Her husband is calling her from his office.
3 A man is reading a newspaper. His wife is calling him from her office.

a

b

c

2 84 **Listen to three conversations.**
Match what the people are doing in the pictures (a-c) with what they *say* they are doing (1-3).

1 "I'm making dinner."
2 "I'm doing my homework."
3 "I'm buying fish for dinner."

SPEAKING

1 **Work with a partner. Complete the conversations with your own ideas.**

a

A: Where are you?
B: I'm on the train.
A: Where / go? *Where are you going?*
B: *I'm going to Chicago.*

b

C: What are you doing, Dad?
D: I'm making dinner.
C: What / make? ______________
D: ______________

c

E: What are you doing?
F: I'm listening to music.
E: What / listen to? ______________
F: ______________

2 **Practice your conversations.**

VOCABULARY

1 **Complete the verb phrases with *do*, *play*, *read*, or *make*.**

a ____*do*____ the housework / the laundry

b ______________ coffee / a telephone call

c ______________ soccer / the piano

d ______________ a book / an email

85 **Listen, check, and repeat.**

2 **Make more verb phrases. Use the words in the box.**

dinner   a computer game   a newspaper   your homework

3 **Mime a verb phrase from Exercise 1. Your partner says what you are doing.**

GRAMMAR

1 **Put the words in the correct order.**

a How often / sneakers / wear / you / do ? *How often do you wear sneakers?*
b laundry / How often / do / the / do / you ?
c you / wear / a hat / do / How often ?

2 **Work with a partner. Ask and answer the questions in Exercise 1.**

How often ...?

How often do you drink coffee?
Every morning.
Every day.
Every week.
Never.

3 86 **Listen and choose the correct adverb of frequency.**

a ~~usually~~ / always
b not usually / sometimes
c never / always
d sometimes / usually
e not usually / usually

4 **Complete the sentences about you with an adverb of frequency.**

a I _____ wear blue jeans.
b I _____ wear a hat.
c I _____ read a book in the evening.
d I _____ cook dinner.

Compare with a partner.

Adverbs of frequency

100% ↑
always
usually
sometimes
not usually
never
0% ↓

LANGUAGE FOR LIFE

1 87 **Read and listen to the conversation. Match it to picture *a*, *b*, or *c*.**

Sales clerk: Can I help you?
Customer: I'm looking for a dress.
Sales clerk: A dress.
Customer: Yes, a dress.
Sales clerk: What size are you?
Customer: It's for my wife.
Sales clerk: What size is she?
Customer: I think she's medium.
Sales clerk: What color?
Customer: Red.
Sales clerk: Do you like this one?
Customer: How much is it?
Sales clerk: It's $500.
Customer: And how much is the blue dress over there?
Sales clerk: It's $90.
Customer: I prefer the blue dress.

2 88 **Listen and repeat the expressions.**

- **a** Can I help you?
- **b** I'm looking for a dress.
- **c** What size are you?
- **d** How much is it?
- **e** How much is the blue dress over there?

3 **Work with a partner. Write a similar conversation for one of the other pictures. Practice the conversation.**

Life Skills: Organization

How often do you ...?

1 **Read and complete the questionnaire.**

How organized are you?			
	How often do you ...		
1	answer all your emails by the end of the day?		
	☐ always	☐ sometimes	☐ never
2	keep an updated weekly planner?		
	☐ always	☐ sometimes	☐ never
3	tidy your workspace at the end of every day?		
	☐ always	☐ sometimes	☐ never
4	put all your documents and files into folders?		
	☐ always	☐ sometimes	☐ never
5	arrive on time for meetings?		
	☐ always	☐ sometimes	☐ never
6	go home on time?		
	☐ always	☐ sometimes	☐ never

How to score:	
never	1
sometimes	2
always	3
0-8	not organized
9-14	quite organized but could improve
15-18	very organized

2 **What can you change? Discuss with your partner.**

MACMILLAN LIFE SKILLS

6 Vocabulary Extra

Colors

1 Match the colors with the words.

_______ purple
_______ gray
_______ black
_______ white
_______ pink
_______ green
_______ yellow
_______ orange
_______ brown
_______ red
_______ blue

Clothes

1 Match the pictures with the words.

_______ boots
_______ a dress
_______ a hat
_______ a jacket
_______ jeans
_______ pants
_______ a shirt
_______ shoes
_______ a skirt
_______ sneakers
_______ a suit
_______ a tank top
_______ a tie
_______ a T-shirt

2 Work with a partner. Cover the words. Look at the clothes. Ask and answer the questions.

What's this?

It's a skirt.

What color is it?

It's blue.

Review B

GRAMMAR

Grammar Extra: pages 60 and 61

1 **Match the times with the same meaning.**

1 It's a quarter to six.
2 It's twenty after eleven.
3 It's ten to five.
4 It's ten after four.
5 It's twenty-five to seven.

a It's six thirty-five.

b It's four ten.

c It's eleven twenty.

d It's five forty-five.

e It's four fifty.

Compare your answers with a partner.

2 **Complete the description of Aiko's day. Use the verbs in the box in the correct form.**

finish get get go go have have have ~~work~~ work

Aiko's Day

Aiko (1) works for an airline. She (2) _____ up at ten thirty in the morning. She (3) _____ breakfast at a quarter to eleven. She (4) _____ to work at a quarter after eleven. She (5) _____ lunch at a quarter to two. She (6) _____ for six more hours. She (7) _____ dinner at nine o'clock in the evening. She (8) _____ work at a quarter to ten. She (9) _____ home at eleven thirty at night. She (10) _____ to bed at one o'clock in the morning.

3 **Complete the sentences with *There's* or *There are*.**

a There are some good restaurants.
b __________ a park.
c __________ a theater.
d __________ some hotels.

Rewrite the sentences as questions.

a *Are there any good restaurants?*
b *Is there _____?*

4 **Put the adverbs of frequency in order (1-5).**

~~always~~ sometimes never not usually usually

1 always 2 __________ 3 __________
4 __________ 5 __________

5 **Complete the sentences with the verbs in the box. Use the present progressive.**

drink eat read sleep ~~talk~~ work

a Alice is talking on the telephone.
b Bella __________ a cup of coffee.
c Chris __________ a newspaper.
d Delia __________ at her computer.
e Ed __________ a sandwich.
f Frank __________ in his favorite chair.

VOCABULARY

1 Complete the names of the jobs (a–f).

a t*a*x*i* dr*i*v*e*r
b d_ct_r
c l_wy_r
d _rt_st
e j_ _rn_l_st
f fl_ght _tt_nd_nt

2 Complete the questions with the phrases in the box.

get home ~~get up~~ go to work have lunch

On weekdays, ...

a what time do you  *get up*?

b what time do you  __________?

c what time do you  __________?

d what time do you  __________?

Work with a partner. Ask and answer the questions.

3 Complete the crossword with the words for places (1–9) in a city.

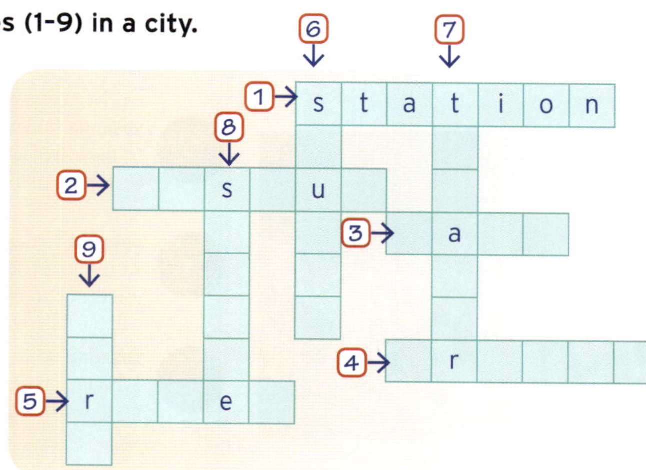

4 Complete the sentences using the pictures and words in the box.

~~red~~ black pink blue

a She's wearing a *red* *dress*.
b He's wearing __________ __________.
c Tom's wearing a __________ __________.
d Maria's wearing a __________ __________.

PRONUNCIATION

1 Look at some words from Units 4–6. Say the words and add them to the table.

~~jacket~~ ~~Brazil~~ taxi ~~France~~ gets ~~museum~~ musician o'clock watches jeans Madrid relaxes

A: ■	B: ■ ▪	C: ▪ ■	D: ▪ ■ ▪
France	*jacket*	*Brazil*	*museum*

2 Underline the stressed syllable in each word.

89 **Listen, check, and repeat.**

READING & LISTENING

1 90 **Read the text. <u>Underline</u> the correct information.**

a Sosanna lives in: (1) the USA (2) the UK (3) Mexico
b Sosanna has: (1) a dog (2) a house (3) a daughter
c Sosanna usually works at: (1) a school (2) a hotel (3) a club
d In the afternoon, Sosanna: (1) sleeps (2) plays the guitar (3) plays the piano
e Sosanna usually goes to the club: (1) after dinner (2) before dinner (3) after *The Simpsons*

Home About

Tweets	Following	Followers	Likes
14.7K	2,024	10,687	1,914

Follow

Sosanna
@sosannastar

Hi, I'm Sosanna. I'm a musician. I sing R&B at clubs and festivals across America. I live in a big apartment here in New York, with my husband Ricky, and my daughter, Noelle.

Tweets **Tweets & replies** **Media**

sosanna @sosannastar • 3h
Some fans asked me about my day. So here is a little bit about myself. (1/6)

sosanna @sosannastar • 2h
On weekdays, we get up early and have breakfast. Ricky goes to work at 7:00 a.m. He's a lawyer and works on Lexington Avenue. I take Noelle to school at 8:00 a.m. (2/6)

sosanna @sosannastar • 2h
After that busy morning, I go back to bed and sleep! Yes, really! At 11:30 a.m. I get up and have lunch. (3/6)

sosanna @sosannastar • 1h
In the afternoon, I play on the piano and I listen to music. Noelle gets home at 4:00 p.m. and we always relax and watch TV. Noelle loves The Simpsons. (4/6)

sosanna @sosannastar • 30m
At 6:00 p.m. Ricky usually gets home and we have dinner. Then I get ready for a concert. I usually go to the club by taxi. (5/6)

sosanna @sosannastar • 10m
I usually finish work at midnight and go home to bed. I don't party much! On weekends, I finish work at 1:00 a.m. or 2 a.m. I work hard but I love my job! (6/6)

2 91 **Listen to the conversation. Are the sentences true or false?**

a Dan Harvey works for a music website.
b Dan Harvey is in London.
c It's three o'clock in the afternoon in London.
d It's eight o'clock in the morning in New York.
e Sosanna speaks Spanish.
f Sosanna usually gets up at eleven thirty.

3 **Listen again and complete the information about Sosanna.**

Sosanna

Star information

Name:	Sosanna
Lives:	New York City
Works:	
Speaks:	
Favorite musician:	
Favorite color:	
Favorite city:	
Favorite food:	

WRITING & SPEAKING

1 Complete the rules for *and* and *but* with the examples in the box.

a You use *and* to join similar ideas. For example:
+ / + I play the piano and I play the guitar.

b You use *but* to join contrasting ideas. For example:
+ / - ______________________
- / + ______________________

> I speak English, but I don't speak Spanish.
> I play the piano and I play the guitar.
> I don't have a sister, but I do have a brother.

2 Join the pairs of sentences using *and* or *but*.

a I watch TV. I relax. I watch TV and I relax.
b She has a computer. She has a camera.
c I speak English. I don't speak Chinese.
d I eat fish. I don't eat meat.
e We get up. We have breakfast.
f I play the piano. I play the guitar.

3 Complete the sentences about yourself. Use the information about Sosanna's day on page 52 to help you.

______ @______
Hi, I'm ______. I'm a ______. I live ______.

______ @______ 10m
On weekdays, I ______ in the morning and I ______. [1/4]

______ @______ 5m
After that, I ______ and I ______. [2/4]

______ @______ 3m
In the evening, I ______ and I ______. [3/4]

______ @______ 2m
On weekends, I ______ but I don't ______. [4/4]

4 Work with a partner. Ask questions with the question forms in the box.

> Where do you ...? Who's your ...? What do you ...? What's your ...?

Name: Paula da Silva
Lives: Rio de Janeiro
Works:
Speaks:
Favorite musician:
Favorite color:
Favorite city:
Favorite food:

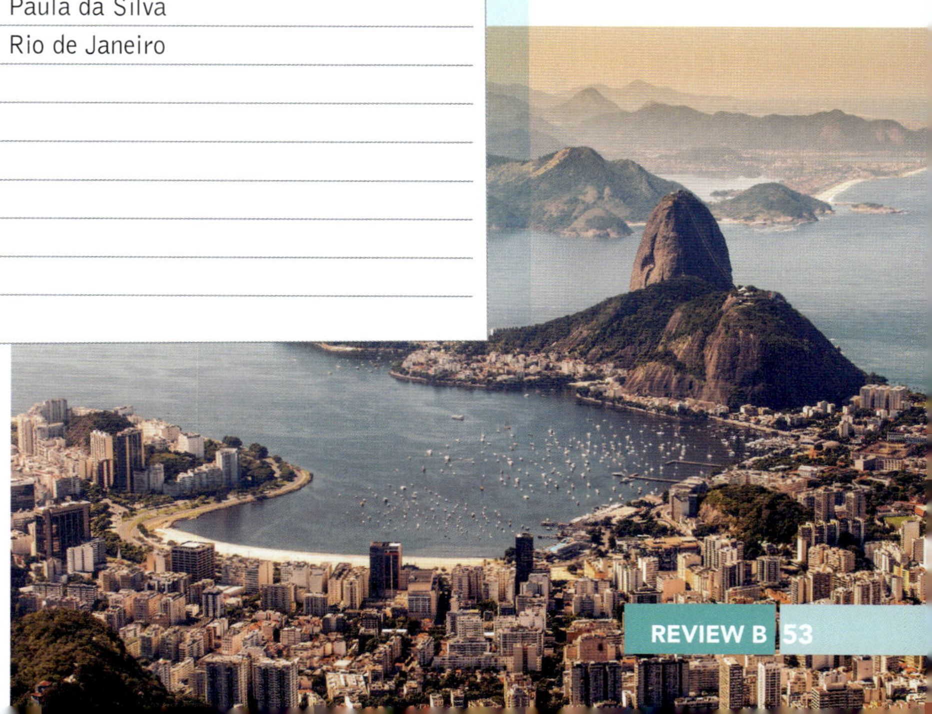

5 Write about your partner using the information in their profile in Exercise 4.

Paula da Silva lives in Rio de Janeiro. She ...

Pairwork: Student A

UNIT 1

Ask Student B and write the missing names.

1 ______________ 2 Beyoncé Knowles-Carter 3 ______________ 4 Jennifer Lawrence 5 ______________ 6 Chris Pratt

Number 1. What's his name?

____

Can you spell that?

UNIT 2

Ask Student B and write the missing countries.

a Ed Sheeran is from *Britain*.
b The Kardashians are from *the USA*.
c Neymar is from ______________.
d Salma Hayek is from ______________.
e Angela Merkel is from ______________.
f Jay-Z and Beyoncé are from ______________.

Is Ed Sheeran from Germany?

Are the Kardashians from the USA?

UNIT 3

The people in the pictures are in your family. Invent their names and tell Student B about them.

This is Rosa. She's my mother. This is Roberto. He's her boyfriend. He's fifty-three.

UNIT 4

Write two sentences for each job.

a

b

c

a I'm a sales clerk. I work in a store.

Ask questions to find out Student B's jobs.

Do you work in an office?
Are you a personal assistant?

UNIT 5

Don't look at Student B's picture. Ask questions to find out what is similar and what is different about your pictures. Use the words in the box or your own ideas.

buildings, a house, cars, a church, people, a river, a square, a statue, stores, street

Is there a river in your picture?

Yes, there is.

Are there any buildings in your picture?

Yes, there are.

UNIT 6

Describe one woman to Student B. Say what she's wearing and what she's doing. Student B says which woman you are describing.

a

b

c

d

Pairwork: Student B

UNIT 1

Ask Student A and write the missing names.

1 

2 

3 

4 

5 

6 

1	2	3	4	5	6
Dwayne Johnson	____________	Scarlett Johansson	____________	John Legend	____________

Number 2. What's her name?

____

Can you spell that?

UNIT 2

Ask Student A and write the missing countries.

1 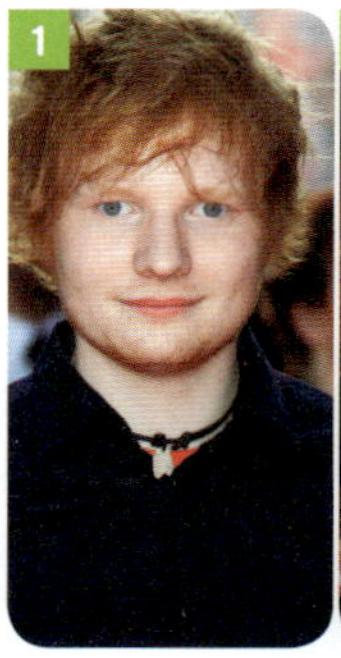

2 

3 

4 

5 

6 

a Ed Sheeran is from ________________..
b The Kardashians are from ________________.
c Neymar is from *Brazil*.
d Salma Hayek is from ________________.
e Angela Merkel is from ________________.
f Jay-Z and Beyoncé are from *the USA*.

Is Neymar from Brazil?

Are Jay-Z and Beyoncé from the USA?

UNIT 3

The people in the pictures are in your family. Invent their names and tell Student A about them.

a 

b 

c 

This is Alan. He's my brother, and this is his wife. Her name's Cherie. This is their daughter, and her name's Lily. She's ten.

UNIT 4

Write two sentences for each job.

a

b

c

a I'm a doctor. I work in a hospital.

Ask questions to find out Student A's jobs.

Do you work in an office?
Are you a personal assistant?

UNIT 5

Don't look at Student A's picture. Ask questions to find out what is similar and what is different about your pictures. Use the words in the box or your own ideas.

buildings a house cars a church
people a river a square a statue
stores street

Is there a statue in your picture?

No, there isn't.

Are there any people in your picture?

Yes, there are.

UNIT 6

Describe one woman to Student A. Say what she's wearing and what she's doing. Student A says which woman you are describing.

a

b

c

d

Grammar Extra

UNIT 1: Nouns

Regular forms

Singular	Plural	Spelling
a pen	pens	Add *s*.
a bus	bus**es**	Add *es* after *ch, sh, s, x*.
a dictionary	dictionar**ies**	Delete *y* and add *ies* after a consonant + *y*.

Irregular forms

Singular	Plural
a person	people
a child	children
a man	men
a woman	women

***a* or *an*?**
You use ***a*** with a singular noun: ***It's a pen.*** (NOT ~~*It's pen.*~~*)*
You use ***a*** before a consonant sound: ***a pen, a bus.***
You use ***an*** before a vowel sound: *an apple, an exercise*

this/that

Singular	What's **this**?	**It**'s a **dictionary**.
Plural	What are **these**?	**They**'re **dictionaries**.

You use *this* to refer to a singular noun.

You use *these* to refer to a plural noun.

UNIT 2: *be*: simple present

Affirmative	Negative
I**'m**	I**'m not**
You**'re**	You **aren't**
He**'s**/She**'s**/It**'s** Mexican.	He/She/It **isn't** Argentinian.
We**'re**	We **aren't**
They**'re**	They **aren't**

Question	**Answer** Yes	**Answer** No
Am I	Yes, I **am**.	No, I**'m not**.
Are you	Yes, you **are**.	No, you **aren't**.
Is he/she/it English?	Yes, he/she/it **is**.	No, he/she/it **isn't**.
Are we	Yes, we **are**.	No, we **aren't**.
Are they	Yes, they **are**.	No, they **aren't**.

In questions, you put *be* before the subject. *Are you English? / Is Neymar Brazilian?* (NOT ~~*You are English?*~~ */* ~~*Neymar is Brazilian?*~~*)*

UNIT 3: Possessive determiners

Subject pronoun	Possessive determiner	
I	my	This is **my** family.
you	your	Where are **your** books?
he	his	Charles and **his** wife.
she	her	Lindy and **her** husband.
it	its	What's **its** name?
we	our	This is **our** house.
they	their	We are **their** parents.

You use the same possessive determiner for singular and plural.
Our family / Our friends (NOT ~~*Ours friends*~~). You use **his** for a man and **her** for a woman.
Bill and his wife = Bill's wife. *Hillary and her husband* = Hillary's husband.

Possessive *'s* and *s'*

You use *'s* for one person.
My brother's school
(= I have one brother.)
You use *s'* for more than one person.
My brothers' school
= (I have two or more brothers.)

UNIT 1: Exercises

1 Put the words in the correct order.

a It's / pen / a . *It's a pen.*
b book / a / It's .
c a / computer / It's .
d It's / bus / a .
e passport / It's / a .
f dictionary / a / It's .

2 Rewrite the sentences in Exercise 1 in the plural.

a *They're pens.*

3 Look at the pictures. Write questions and answers.

a *What's this? It's a bag.*
b *What are these? They're ...*

a 
b 
c 
d 
e 

UNIT 2: Exercises

1 Write the sentences with contractions.

a I am from Brazil. *I'm from Brazil.*
b You are from Mexico.
c He is from Italy.
d She is from Japan.
e They are from Spain.
f We are international!

2 Write the sentences in Exercise 1 in the negative.

a *I'm not from Brazil.*

3 Make questions.

a The Eiffel Tower is in Buenos Aires.
Is the Eiffel Tower in Buenos Aires?
b Big Ben is in New York City.
c Petronas Towers are in Cairo.
d The Brooklyn Bridge is in London.
e The Kremlin is in Paris.
f The Pyramids are in the USA.

UNIT 3: Exercises

1 Complete the table.

Subject pronoun	Possessive determiner
I	(1) *my*
you	(2) _____
(3)_____	his
she	her
(4) _____	its
we	(5) _____
they	(6) _____

2 Look at the pictures. Underline the correct form.

a This is my **parent's** / **parents'** house.
b This is my **mother's** / **mothers'** car.
c These are my **father's** / **fathers'** cars.
d This is my **sister's** / **sisters'** college.
e These are my **sister's** / **sisters'** boyfriends.

a 
b 
c 
d 
e 

UNIT 4: Simple present

Affirmative		Negative	
I		I	
You	**work.**	You	**don't work.**
We		We	
They		They	
He/She/It	**works.**	He/She/It	**doesn't work.**

You use ***do*** to make questions with all verbs for ***I***, ***you***, ***we***, ***they***.
You put ***do*** before the subject. ***Do you work in a school?*** (NOT ~~*You work in a school?*~~)
You use ***does*** to make questions with all verbs for ***he***, ***she***, ***it***.
You put ***does*** before the subject. ***Does she work in a school?*** (NOT ~~*She works in a school?*~~)

Verb	he/she/it	Spelling
live, play, work	live**s**, play**s**, work**s**	Add *s*.
watch, finish	watch**es**, finish**es**	Add *es* after *ch*, *sh*, *s*, *x*.
study	stud**ies**	Delete *y* and add *ies* after a consonant + *y*.
do, go, have	does, goes, has	Irregular forms

be
You don't use *do* or *does* with *be*. ***Are*** *you English?* (NOT ~~*Do you are English?*~~)

UNIT 5: *there is/there are; some/any*

	Affirmative	Negative
Singular	**There's** a school.	**There isn't** a hospital.
Plural	**There are** some people.	**There aren't** any bars.

	Question	**Answer** Yes	**Answer** No
Singular	Is there a **doctor**?	Yes, there **is**.	No, there **isn't**.
Plural	Are there **any hotels**?	Yes, there **are**.	No, there **aren't**.

some/any
With plurals, you use ***some*** in affirmative sentences. ***There are*** some ***people.***
With plurals, you use ***any*** in negative sentences. ***There aren't*** any ***bars. Are there*** any ***hotels?***

UNIT 6: Present Progressive

Affirmative	Negative
I**'m**	I**'m not**
You**'re**	You **aren't**
He**'s**/She**'s**/It**'s** **working.**	He/She/It **isn't working.**
We**'re**	We **aren't**
They**'re**	They **aren't**

Spelling

Verbs that end in **e**: *live* ⟶ ***living***
Verbs that end in one vowel + one consonant: *run* ⟶ ***running***

Question	**Answer** Yes	**Answer** No
Am I	Yes, I **am**.	No, I**'m not**.
Are you	Yes, you **are**.	No, you **aren't**.
Is he/she/it **working**?	Yes, he/she/it **is**.	No, he/she/it **isn't**.
Are we	Yes, we **are**.	No, we **aren't**.
Are they	Yes, they **are**.	No, they **aren't**.

UNIT 4: Exercises

1 **Write the sentences in the negative.**

a I speak Chinese.
I don't speak Chinese.
b He smokes.
c I drink beer.
d She has a car.
e I live with my parents.
f We work in the city.
g It plays music.
h They listen to music.

2 **Write the simple present forms for he/she/it.**

a do *does*
b finish
c get
d go
e have
f like
g study
h watch

3 **Pete is a mailman. Read about his weekdays. Underline the verbs in the simple present.**

4 **Compare your weekdays with Pete's. Write sentences.**

a *Pete gets up at 4:30 a.m. I get up at 7:00 a.m.*
b *Pete goes to work ...*

"I get up at 4:30 a.m. I go to work at 5:30 a.m. and I finish work at about 1:00 p.m. I get home at 2:00 p.m. and have lunch at 3:00 p.m. I go to the gym in the afternoon. I have dinner at 7:00 p.m. and I go to bed at about 9:30 p.m."

UNIT 5: Exercises

1 **Match the numbers with the phrases.**

a 7 — minutes in an hour
b 26 — hours in a day
c 60 — days in a week
d 50 — players on a soccer team
e 24 — states in the USA
f 11 — letters in the English alphabet

Write sentences.

a *There are seven days in a week.*

2 **Cross out the incorrect form.**
In our classroom, ...

a there are ~~**any**~~ / **some** dictionaries.
b there's **a** / **an** map of the USA.
c there are **any** / **some** Brazilian students.
d there's **a** / **an** old CD player.
e there's **a** / **an** computer.
f there are **any** / **some** pictures.

3 **Write negative sentences for Exercise 2.**

a *In our classroom, there aren't any dictionaries.*

Check (✓) the sentences in Exercises 2 and 3 that are true for your classroom.

UNIT 6: Exercises

1 **Complete the table.**

A	B	C
speak *speaking*	have *having*	sit *sitting*
do ______	make ______	run ______
play ______	write ______	get up ______

2 **Write the *ing* form of these verbs and add them to the table.**

come dance go learn read sleep stop study take work

3 **Think about your friends and family. What are they doing now? Write three sentences.**

My father's working.

4 **Write a question and answer for each picture.**

a *What's she doing? She's running.*

Audio script

Unit 0

2

Ask.
Answer.
Listen.
Speak.
Point.
Look.
Write.
Read.

3

a Look at the pictures.
b Listen and repeat.
c Practice the conversation.
d Read the text.
e Compare your answers.
f Check your answers.

4

a Complete.
b Circle.
c Underline.
d Check.
e Cross out.
f Match.

Unit 1

5

Woman: Hello. I'm Sandra. What's your name?
Man: Hello, Sandra. My name's Diego. Nice to meet you.

6

a What's his name?
His name's Daniel Craig.
b What's her name?
Her name's Naomi Harris.

7

zero / oh
one
two
three
four
five
six
seven
eight
nine
ten

8

a one, two, three, four, five
b five, four, three, two, one
c two, four, six, eight, ten
d one, three, five, seven, nine

9

a What's your cell phone number?
302 741 6995
b What's your home number?
240 856 3213

10

1 a bag
2 a computer
3 books
4 pens
5 keys
6 a cell phone
7 a passport
8 a camera

11

a What's this? It's a bag.
b What's this? It's a computer.
c What are these?
They're books.
d What are these?
They're pens.
e What are these?
They're keys.
f What's this? It's a cell phone.
g What's this? It's a passport.
h What's this? It's a camera.

12

(G = Greg; T = Tina)
G: Hey, Tina.
T: Yes, Greg.
G: What's in your bag?
T: A computer, a camera, three books, a cell phone, er ...my passport .... What's in your bag?
G: A cell phone.
T: Oh. Where's your computer?
G: I don't need one. I have my phone.
T: Where's your camera?
G: I don't need one. I have my phone.
T: Where's your passport?
G: I don't nee ... Passport? Oh, no!

13

A B
C D
E F
G
H I
J K
L M N O
P
Q R
S
T U
V
W
X
Y
Z

14

1 B C D E G P T V Z
2 F L M N S X
3 A H J K
4 Q U W
5 I Y
6 O
7 R

15

1 USA
2 UK
3 VIP
4 OK
5 CNN
6 CIA

16

(R = Receptionist; S = Student)
R: Welcome to The Oxford English School. What's your name?
S: Yolanda.
R: Can you spell that, please?
S: Y-O-L-A-N-D-A.
R: And your last name?
S: C-A-S-T-I-L-L-A.
R: Sorry, can you repeat that, please?

S: C-A-S-T-I-L-L-A.
R: Thank you, Ms. Castilla.
S: Please call me Yolanda.
R: OK. Thank you, Yolanda.

17

a Can you spell that, please?
b Sorry, can you repeat that, please?
c Please call me Yolanda.

Unit 2

18

And now on Rock Star Talent, please welcome...
Number 1 from Mexico!
Number 2 from Germany!
Number 3 from Chile!
Number 4 from Japan!
Number 5 from Brazil!
Number 6 from Spain!

19

1 Mexico
2 Germany
3 Chile
4 Japan
5 Brazil
6 Spain

20

a Is Monika from Germany?
Yes, she is.
No, she isn't.
b Is Rosa from Japan?
Yes, she is.
No, she isn't.
c Is Victor from Chile?
Yes, he is.
No, he isn't.
d Are Andreas and Ana from Brazil?
Yes, they are.
No, they aren't.
e Are you from Spain?
Yes, I am.
No, I'm not.
f Are you and your teacher from Mexico?
Yes, we are.
No, we aren't.

21

a Where are you from?
I'm from Paterna.
It's near Valencia in Spain.
b Where are you from?
We're from Niteroi.
It's near Rio in Brazil.

22

American
Brazilian
British
Chilean
German
Japanese
Mexican
Spanish

23

a She's British.
b It's Mexican.
c He's Spanish.
d They're Brazilian.
e They're German.
f They're Japanese.

24

eleven
twelve
thirteen
fourteen
fifteen
sixteen
seventeen
eighteen
nineteen

twenty
thirty
forty
fifty
sixty
seventy
eighty
ninety

one hundred

25

a twenty-one
twenty-two
twenty-three

b thirty-four
thirty-five
thirty-six

c forty-seven
forty-eight
forty-nine

d one hundred and eleven
one hundred and twelve
one hundred and thirteen

26

a Connect thirty, sixty-six, and fourteen.
Connect thirteen, thirty, and seventy-four.

b Connect fifteen, fifty, and ninety-nine.
Connect fifteen and twenty-four.
Connect fifty and eighty-three.
Connect ninety-nine and one hundred and ninety-nine.

c Connect eighteen, seventy, and seventy-nine.
Connect eighteen, eighty, and one hundred and sixty.
Connect one hundred and sixty, thirty-eight, and twenty-nine.

27

1 euros
2 pounds
3 dollars
4 real

28

a Three dollars and fifty cents.
b Five pounds thirty.
c Seventy euros seventy-five.
d Nineteen ninety-nine reais.
e Eighty euros twenty.
f Forty pounds forty.
g One hundred and sixteen dollars.

29

a How much is a cappuccino in New York City?
Five dollars.

b How much is a hamburger in Mexico City?
Three fifty.

c How much is a movie ticket in London?
Sixteen dollars and fifty cents.

d How much is a night in a 3-star hotel in Tokyo?
Two hundred and ten dollars.

30

a How much is a cappuccino in New York City?
b How much is a hamburger in London?
c How much is a movie ticket in Tokyo?
d How much is a night in a 3-star hotel in Mexico?

31

a
Man: How much is this?
Woman: Twenty dollars fifty.
Man: OK, thanks.

b
Boy: How much are these?
Man: Nine dollars.
Boy: OK, thanks.

c
Woman: How much is this?
Woman: Eight euros twenty.
Woman: OK, thanks.

d
Man: How much are these?
Man: One hundred and seventy-five dollars.
Man: Oh! OK, no thanks.

32

a How much is this?
b How much are these?
c OK, thanks.

33

a British
b Japanese
c American
d German
e Spanish
f Mexican

34

a It's the Rio Carnival in Brazil
b It's the Thanksgiving Parade in the USA.
c It's Oktoberfest in Germany.
d It's the Day of the Dead in Mexico.

Unit 3

35

This is my family and this is me.
My name's Luisa.
This is my dad.
His name's Lucas.
This is my mom.
Her name's Julia.
This is my brother.
His name's Bruno.
This is my baby sister.
Her name's Ana.
These are my grandparents.
My grandma's name is Maria, and my grandpa's name is Victor.

36

1 father (dad)
2 mother (mom)
3 brother
4 sister
5 grandmother (grandma)
6 grandfather (grandpa)

37

a How old are you?
I'm six.
b How old is your brother?
He's four.
c How old is your sister?
She's one.
d How old are your mother and father?
They're forty-two.
e How old is your grandmother?
She's sixty-eight.
f How old is your grandfather?
He's seventy.

38

a Julia is Luisa's mother.
b Bruno is Luisa's brother.
c Victor is Luisa's grandfather.
d Ana is Luisa's sister.
e Lucas is Luisa's father.
f Maria is Luisa's grandmother.

39

(V = Victor; F = Friend)
V: This is on vacation in Mexico. This is me, with my wife.
F: Maria?
V: Yes, that's Maria. And this is my daughter getting married.
F: Aah, nice. What's her name?
V: Julia, and her husband's name is Lucas.
F: And are these your grandchildren?
V: This is my granddaughter Ana.
F: How old is she?
V: She's one. And this is Luisa. She's six.

40

mother
daughter
grandmother
granddaughter
sister
wife

father
son
grandfather
grandson
brother
husband

parents
children
grandparents
grandchildren

41

a
Hello to the Smiths!
Who's on the red carpet? It's the Smith family!
Fresh Prince of Bel Air actor and movie star, Will Smith is married to actor Jada Pinkett-Smith.
They have two children.
And their children are stars now!
Jaden Smith is an actor and singer, and he was in the movies *Karate Kid* and *After Earth*.
Jaden has a little sister, Willow.
She is young, but she has a hit song already, with *Whip My Hair*.
Will's oldest son Trey, from his first marriage, is a DJ in Los Angeles.

b
It's a Cyrus family event.
That is the Cyrus family at the music awards.
Father, Billy Ray Cyrus, a famous singer, enjoyed the evening with his wife, Leticia.
Billy and Leticia have three children.
Miley Cyrus is a big TV and music star, and her sister, Noah, is also a pop singer.

42

a Jada Pinkett-Smith and her daughter are actors.
b Billy Ray Cyrus and his daughters are singers.
c Jaden, Willow, and their parents are all famous stars.
d Miley Cyrus says, "My sister and I are now singers. Our parents are so proud!"
e Noah Cyrus is happy to be a singer like her sister and her father.

43

a I have one brother.
b My parents have a dog.
c My mother has three brothers.
d My grandparents have two houses.
e My husband and I have two children.
f My father has a Japanese car.

44

a He's a teacher. She's an actor.
b He has a Samsung Galaxy. She has an iPhone.
c He has a Japanese car. She has an American car.

45

an + vowel sound
an Oreo cookie
an English dictionary
an Android cell phone
an Apple computer
an American grandmother

a + consonant sound
a brother
a dog
a Gucci bag
a passport
a sister

46

Tim: This is Anna. She's my sister.
Gerry: Nice to meet you. I'm Gerry.
Anna: Nice to meet you.
Rob: This is Sophia. She's Brazilian.
Becky: Nice to meet you. I'm Rob's wife.
Sophia: Nice to meet you.

47

a This is Anna.
b Nice to meet you.
c I'm Gerry.

48

Anna: This is Tim.
Sophia: Nice to meet you. I'm Sophia.
Tim: Nice to meet you.

49

a
Anna: Who's this?
Bridget: This is my grandmother, Anna. She's ninety-three.
Anna: Really?
Bridget: Yes. She looks amazing, doesn't she?

b
Luis: And who's this?
Fran: Oh, this is my sister, Esther. She's a doctor at the city hospital.
Luis: Is that right?
Fran: Yes. She's very smart

c
Shen: Who's this in the photo?
Jenny: He's my grandfather, Ben. He's seventy-two. He runs marathons.
Shen: No way!
Jenny: I know. We all think he's crazy...

d
Pippa: And who's the boy?
Tom: Ah, that's my son, Will.
Pippa: Where is he?
Tom: He's at his grandparents.
Pippa: Oh, I see.

50

a normal
I see.
b strong
That's amazing.
c normal
That's interesting.
d strong
No way!
e strong
Really?
f normal
Right.
g strong
You're kidding!

REVIEW A

51

A adjective, Mexico, granddaughter, singular
B computer, description, possessive, Chilean
C Japanese, seventeen

52

(R = Receptionist; PE = Paula Espinoza)
R: Good afternoon, ma'am.
PE: Good afternoon. How much is one night at this hotel?
R: One night is $190.
PE: Oh, OK. One night, please.
R: Sure, What's your first name?
PE: Paula.
R: Can you spell that?
PE: P-A-U-L-A.
R: And your last name?
PE: Espinoza.
R: Espinoza? Can you spell that, please?
PE: E-S-P-I-N-O-Z-A.
R: Sorry, can you repeat that?
PE: E-S-P-I-N-O-Z-A.
R: Thank you. Do you have a telephone number?
PE: Yes, it's 55-5130-5872.
R: Are you from the USA, Ms. Espinoza?
PE: No, I'm not. I'm Mexican. I'm from Mexico City.
R: Your passport number, please, Ms. Espinoza?
PE: It's G489-798-23
R: Sorry, can you repeat that, please?
PE: It's G489-798-23
R: Thank you. Here's your key. Your room number is 48.

Unit 4

53

a I live in an old house. I live with my parents.
b I have one brother. I have an old car.
c I work in an office. I work for Apple.
d I like swimming.
e I speak English. I speak Japanese.
f I eat meat. I eat vegetables.

54

a Do you speak Chinese?
Yes, I do.
No, I don't
b Do you smoke?
Yes, I do.
No, I don't.

c Do you and your family live in a city?
Yes, we do.
No, we don't.
d Do your friends eat soccer?
Yes, they do.
No, they don't.
e Do you eat meat?
Yes, I do.
No, I don't.
f Do your parents have a dog?
Yes, they do.
No, they don't.

55
a Where do you live?
b Where do you work?
c What languages do you speak?
d What food do you like?
e What music do you like?
f What sports do you like?

56
a He's a lawyer.
b He's a taxi driver.
c He's a soccer player.
d She's a pilot.
e She's an artist.
f He's a musician.

57
a I'm a flight attendant.
b I'm a doctor.
c I'm a personal assistant.
d I'm a farmer.
e I'm a sales clerk.
f I'm a journalist.

58
(I = Interviewer; M = Man; W = Woman)

1
I: Excuse me. What do you do?
W: I'm a teacher.
I: What's your dream job?
W: Oh, um, musician.
I: Thank you.

2
I: Excuse me. What do you do?
M: I'm a lawyer.
I: And what's your dream job?
M: My dream job? Soccer player.
I: Thank you.

3
I: Excuse me. What do you do?
M: I'm a taxi driver.
I: What's your dream job?
M: Um, pilot. Yes, pilot.
I: Thank you.

4
I: Excuse me. What do you do?
W: I'm a student.
I: What's your dream job?
W: Oh, I don't know. Um, doctor. No, DJ. No, doctor.
I: Doctor?
W: No, DJ.
I: DJ?
W: Yes, DJ.
I: Thank you.

5
I: Excuse me. What do you do?
W: I'm an actor.
I: What's your dream job?
W: My dream job? Actor!
I: Thank you.

59
Sunday
Monday
Tuesday
Wednesday
Thursday
Friday
Saturday

60
a get up
b go to bed
c have breakfast
d have lunch
e have dinner
f go to work
g finish work
h get home

61
Hey, fans! Happy Wednesday! This is my routine during the week. I get up early, have breakfast, and take my son to school. Then I go to the gym – have to stay fit and healthy. After that I go to work in a recording studio. Right now, we're in Sky Studios. It's a beautiful place. After I finish work, I go home and have dinner with my family. We have two young children, River and Lake, so we all go to bed early. Nice!

Hey, guys! Another Saturday night – who wants to have some fun? On Saturdays, I go to bed in the afternoon and then I go to work. I work all night in the club. I love DJing all night! My favorite club is Club Liquid in Sao Paulo, but I work in clubs all around the world. Visit my website www.djluiz.com for club dates. I work hard, but I also have a good time. So, who's ready for a BIG night?

62
a
Does he go to the gym on weekdays?
Yes, he does.
No, he doesn't.

b
Does he have children?
Yes, he does.
No, he doesn't.

c
Does he go to bed in the evening on Saturdays?
Yes, he does.
No, he doesn't.

d
Does he work in clubs all around the world?
Yes, he does.
No, he doesn't.

e
Does he like his job?
Yes, he does.
No, he doesn't.

63
A
do - does
get - gets
go - goes
have - has

B
finish - finishes
relax - relaxes
teach - teaches
watch - watches

64
a What time is it in San Francisco?
It's four o'clock in the morning.
b What time is it in Buenos Aires?
It's eight o'clock in the morning.
c What time is it in London?
It's noon, twelve p.m.

- **d** What time is it in Moscow? It's three o'clock in the afternoon.
- **e** What time is it in Hong Kong? It's eight o'clock in the evening.
- **f** What time is it in Wellington? Twelve a.m. It's midnight.

65

- **a** Four a.m. It's four o'clock in the morning.
- **b** Eight a.m. It's eight o'clock in the morning.
- **c** Twelve p.m. It's noon.
- **d** Three p.m. It's three o'clock in the afternoon.
- **e** Eight p.m. It's eight o'clock in the evening.
- **f** Twelve a.m. It's midnight.

66

- **a** It's two twenty-five.
  It's twenty-five after two.
- **b** It's seven fifty.
  It's ten to eight.
- **c** It's three thirty-five.
  It's twenty-five to four.
- **d** It's ten fifteen.
  It's a quarter after ten.
- **e** It's five-oh-five.
  It's five after five.
- **f** It's twelve forty-five.
  It's a quarter to one.

67

(Mr. E = Mr. Edwards; J = John)

Mr. E: Hello.
J: Good morning! Is this Mr. Edwards?
Mr. E: Who is this?
J: It's John from New York.
Mr. E: What time is it in New York, John?
J: It's 8:30 in the morning.
Mr. E: Oh. Do you know what time it is in Sydney, John?
J: Er, no. What time is it in Sydney, Mr. Edwards?
Mr. E: It's 11:30 ... p.m.
J: Oh, good evening, Mr. Edwards.
Mr. E: Goodnight, John.

68

- **a** Good morning.
- **b** Good afternoon.
- **c** Good evening.
- **d** Goodnight.

Unit 5

69

1. The Chrysler Building
2. Grand Central Station
3. Central Park
4. The Statue of Liberty
5. Times Square
6. The Metropolitan Museum
7. Brooklyn Bridge

70

a bridge
a building
a lake
a museum
a park
a river
a square
a station
a statue
a theater

71

a
My name's Rick.
I love Brooklyn.
I live in an old apartment in Williamsburg, near the river.
I work in an office near the Williamsburg Bridge.
There are so many great places in Williamsburg - rooftop bars, cool movie theaters, and funky shops.
There is a great atmosphere.

b
I'm Betty.
I love New York and I love Brooklyn.
I live in a modern apartment in the Dumbo area of Brooklyn, near the Brooklyn Bridge.
My office is near my apartment so there is no need to commute.
Dumbo is new but it's growing fast.
There is a great bookstore near my office - great for a visit at lunchtime.
There is also a ferry stop in Dumbo to travel up the river.

c
My name's Sam.
I love New York. I live in a brownstone in the center of Prospect Heights.
I work in an art gallery near the Brooklyn Public Library.
There are many cool things to do in Prospect Heights.
There are museums, and there is a great park to relax in.
There is also the Brooklyn Nets basketball arena.

72

- **a** There's a zoo.
- **b** There are 36 bridges.
- **c** There are three restaurants.
- **d** There are six cafés.
- **e** There's a museum.
- **f** There are 25 million visitors every year.

73

A
There's a park.
There are some trees.
There are some statues.
There are some people.

B
There's a street.
There are some cars.
There are some buses.
There are some people.

74

- **a** Is there a station near your house?
  Yes, there is.
  No, there isn't.
- **b** Are there any restaurants near your house?
  Yes, there are.
  No, there aren't.
- **c** Is there a museum in your city?
  Yes, there is.
  No, there isn't.
- **d** Is there a park near your house?
  Yes, there is.
  No, there isn't.
- **e** Are there any hotels in your city?
  Yes, there are.
  No, there aren't.
- **f** Is there a church near your house?
  Yes, there is.
  No, there isn't.

75

- **a** a pharmacy
- **b** an ATM
- **c** a subway station
- **d** a restroom

76

(M = Man; W = Woman)

a

M: Excuse me. Is there a pharmacy near here?
W: A what?
M: A pharmacy.
W: A pharmacy? Er, yes – over there.
M: Thanks.

b

W: Excuse me. Is there a restroom near here?
M: A restroom?
W: Yes, yes, a restroom.
M: A restroom? Near here? No.
W: Oh!

77

a Excuse me.
b Is there a pharmacy near here?
c Yes - over there.

Unit 6

78

black
white
red
blue
green
yellow
gray
pink
orange
brown

79

a

1 a black jacket
2 a white T-shirt
3 blue pants
4 black shoes

b

1 a blue hat
2 a green top
3 a gray skirt
4 purple boots

c

1 a red dress
2 black shoes

d

1 a gray suit
2 a blue tie
3 a blue shirt
4 red and white sneakers

80

Jasmine is wearing a red dress and black shoes.
Kate is wearing a blue hat, a green top, a gray skirt, and purple boots.
Jason is wearing a gray suit, a blue tie, a blue shirt, and red and white sneakers.
Leon is wearing a black jacket, a white T-shirt, blue pants, and black shoes.

81

1 As a student, Kumiko usually wears a T-shirt and jeans, but today is a special day for Kumiko and her friends. Kumiko is graduating from college, so she's wearing a hakama. This is traditional Japanese clothing that students wear for graduation day.

2 Veena and Sita are having fun this weekend in Mumbai, India. It's their friend's wedding, so they are dressing up. Look at those beautiful Indian clothes! They work in a call center. There Veena and Sita usually wear white shirts and black skirts, but today they are dancing at a wedding in beautiful and colorful silk saris.

3 Peter and Stan are Physical Education teachers. They usually wear tracksuits, but not today!
They're going horse racing. Peter and Stan are wearing hats, suit jackets, striped pants, and waistcoats.

82

a Are Lola and Ana wearing black skirts?
Yes, they are.
No, they aren't.

b Are they dancing?
Yes, they are.
No, they aren't.

c Is Peter wearing sneakers?
Yes, he is.
No, he isn't.

d Are Veena and Sita having a great time?
Yes, they are.
No, they aren't.

e Is Kumiko wearing jeans?
Yes, she is.
No, she isn't.

f Is she holding a parasol?
Yes, she is.
No, she isn't.

83

A

Teaching or learning?
Studying or working?
What are you doing?
What are you doing?

B

Eating or drinking?
Sleeping or thinking?
What are you doing?
What are you doing?

C

Running or walking?
Listening and talking?
What are you doing?
What are you doing?

84

a

(H = Husband; W = Wife)

H: Hello, Kate.
W: Oh, hi, honey.
H: Where are you?
W: Oh, um, I'm at the grocery store.
H: What are you buying for dinner?
W: Er, for dinner? Fish. I'm buying fish for dinner.

b

(L = Liza; D = Don)

L: Hello, Don.
D: Oh, hi, Liza.
L: What are you doing?
D: Er, I'm making dinner.
L: Ah, good.

c

(M = Mother; S = Son)

M: Hello.
S: Hi, Mom.
M: What are you doing?
S: Er, I'm doing my homework.
M: Great.

85

a do the housework
do the laundry
b make coffee
make a telephone call
c play soccer
play the piano
d read a book
read an email

86

a She always wears blue jeans.
b I sometimes wear a hat.
c He never does the laundry.
d She usually makes a coffee in the morning.
e I usually wear sneakers.

87

Sales clerk: Can I help you?
Customer: I'm looking for a dress.
Sales clerk: A dress.
Customer: Yes, a dress.
Sales clerk: What size are you?
Customer: It's for my wife.
Sales clerk: What size is she?
Customer: I think she's medium.
Sales clerk: What color?
Customer: Red.
Sales clerk: Do you like this one?
Customer: How much is it?
Sales clerk: It's $500.
Customer: And how much is the blue dress over there?
Sales clerk: It's $90.
Customer: I prefer the blue dress.

88

a Can I help you?
b I'm looking for a dress.
c What size are you?
d How much is it?
e How much is the blue dress over there?

REVIEW B

89

A
France, jeans, gets

B
jacket, taxi, watches

C
Brazil, Madrid, o'clock

D
museum, musician, relaxes

90

Hi, I'm Sosanna. I'm a musician.
I sing R&B at clubs and festivals across America.
I live in a big apartment here in New York, with my husband Ricky, and my daughter, Noelle.

Some fans have asked me about my day.
So here is a a little bit about myself.

On weekdays, we get up early and have breakfast.
Ricky goes to work at 7:00 a.m. He's a lawyer and works on Lexington Avenue.
I take Noelle to school at 8:00 a.m.

After that busy morning, I go back to bed and sleep!
Yes, really!
At 11:30 a.m. I get up and have lunch.

In the afternoon, I play on the piano and I listen to music.
Noelle gets home at 4:00 p.m. and we always relax and watch TV.
Noelle loves ***The Simpsons***.

At 6:00 p.m. Ricky usually gets home and we have dinner.
Then I get ready for a concert.
I usually go to the club by taxi.

I usually finish work at midnight and go home to bed.
I don't party much!
On weekends, I finish work at 1:00 a.m. or 2 a.m.
I work hard but I love my job!

91

(D = Dan Harvey; S = Sosanna)
D: Hello, is this Sosanna?
S: Yes, Sosanna speaking. Who's this?
D: Hi, I'm Dan Harvey. I work for musicexpress.com here in London.
S: Oh, OK. What time is it in London?
D: Er, it's one o'clock in the afternoon.
S: Well, Dan, it's eight o'clock in the morning here.
D: Oh ... er, sorry, Sosanna. Look, can I ask you some questions for our website?
S: Er, yes, OK.
D: So ... where do you live?
S: Here, in New York City.
D: OK. And where do you work?
S: In R&B clubs.
D: OK. What languages do you speak?
S: Er, English ... and Spanish. My husband's Mexican, you know.
D: Oh. Who's your favorite musician?
S: Mavis Staples.
D: OK, could you spell her last name?
S: Sure, it's Staples. S-T-A-P-L-E-S. She's an R&B and gospel singer.
D: Uh huh. And what's your favorite color?
S: Er, um ... red?
D: What's your favorite city? Do you like London. Or L.A.?
S: Er, yes, I do. But I love New York City!
D: Oh. And what's your favorite food?
S: Pasta.
D: OK. And finally, what time do you usually get up?
S: 11:30.
D: Oh, yes, sorry! Thank you, Sosanna! Goodbye!
S: Have a good day!

Notes

Macmillan Education

Companies and representatives throughout the world
American Inside Out Evolution. Student's Book Beginner

D.R. © Macmillan Publishers, S.A. de C.V., 2017
Text D.R. © Sue Kay and Vaughan Jones, 2017
Adapted by Peter Maggs and Catherine Smith / The Content Station team: Simon Campbell, George Wells and Catherine Gray
Macmillan is a registered trademark.
First edition published 2017

ISBN 978-607-473-619-9

Based on New American Inside Out Student's Book Beginner
D.R. © Macmillan Publishers, S.A. de C.V. 2008
Published under license from Macmillan Publishers Ltd.

All rights reserved; no part of this publication may be reproduced, stored in a retrieval system, transmitted in any form, or by any means, electronic, mechanical, photocopying, recording, or otherwise, without the prior written permission of the publishers.

Editorial Manager: Patricia Muradas
Editorial Operations Coordinator: Veronica Teodorov Ferreira
Editor: Cintia Zaitune
Concept design: Martha Tadaieski
Design: Jean Aranha
Page make-up: The Content Station
Illustration: Karen Ahlschläger pp 9, 22, 23, 27, 50;
Gustavo Gialuca pp 14, 20, 26, 36, 42, 48
Graphic Production: Kelly Gobbo
Photographic research: The Content Station
Cover concept and design: Jean Aranha
Cover photo: Giovanni Gagliardi | Dreamstime

The authors and publishers would like to thank the following for permission to reproduce the photographic material:
Dreamstime / Diego Vito Cervo p8, Dreamstime / Faysalfarhan p8 (ask), p8 (answer), p8 (listen), p8 (speak), p8 (point), p8 (look), p8 (write), p8 (read), Dreamstime / Mariusika11 p11(1), Dreamstime / Vadym Soloviov p11(2), Dreamstime / TonyTaylorStock p11(3), Dreamstime / Hallbergsf p11(4), Dreamstime / Maigi p11(5), Dreamstime / Nadezhda1906 p11(6), Dreamstime / Ingrid Prats p11(7), Dreamstime / Winterling p11(8), Dreamstime / Eddydegroot p11(9), Dreamstime / Photographybabak p11(10), Dreamstime / Oleksii Afanasiev p11 (home phone), Dreamstime / Pedro Nogueira p11 (cell phone), Dreamstime / Habrda p12 (bag), Dreamstime / Samystclair p12 (passport), Dreamstime / Panagiotis Risvas p12 (books), Dreamstime / Thatpichai page 12 (phone), Dreamstime / Hangingpixels p12 (camera), Dreamstime / Dmitriy Sladkov p12 (pens), Dreamstime / Nectar3d p12 (keys), Dreamstime / Anton Samsonov p12 (laptop), Dreamstime / Monkey Business Images p13, Dreamstime / Lightkitegirl p14 (book), Dreamstime / Yulia Ryabokon p14 (passport), Dreamstime / Ylivdesign p14 (pens), Dreamstime / Microphoto1981 p14 (laptop), Dreamstime / Serhii Brovko p14 (notebook), Dreamstime / Foxyliam p14 (phone), Dreamstime / Yulia Ryabokon p14 (dictionary), Dreamstime / Lenanet p14(ml), Dreamstime / Robert Kneschke p14(mr), Dreamstime / Vladimir Yudin p15(1), Dreamstime / Andrey Dybrovskiy p15(2), Dreamstime / Ylivdesign p15(3), Dreamstime / Yulia Ryabokon p15(4), Dreamstime / Ylivdesign p15(5), Dreamstime / Gstudioimagen p15(6), Dreamstime / Oleksii Afanasiev p15(7), Dreamstime / Makc76 p15(8), Dreamstime / Ylivdesign p15(9), Dreamstime / Axel Bueckert p15(b), Dreamstime / Ivan Paunovic p16(1 flag), Dreamstime / Anthony Brown p16(2 flag), Dreamstime / Photographerlondon p16(2), Dreamstime / Sarah Nicholl p16(3 flag), Dreamstime / Fckncg p16(4 flag), Dreamstime / Luis Carlos Torres p16(5 flag), Dreamstime / Warrengoldswain p16(5), Dreamstime / Rsnapshotphotos p16(6 flag), Dreamstime / Christian Bertrand p16(flag), Dreamstime / Mileatanasov p17 (ball), Dreamstime / Loopall p17 (box), Dreamstime / Peter Hermes Furian p17(tl), Dreamstime / Iuliia Bereznikova p17(tm), Dreamstime / Norman Chan p17(ml), Dreamstime / Tuomaslehtinen p17(mr), Dreamstime / Christian Bertrand p17(tr), Dreamstime / Warrengoldswain p17(b), Dreamstime / Glowonconcept p18(br), Dreamstime / Brandon Seidel p18 (USA), Dreamstime / Said Tayar Segundo p18 (Brazil), Dreamstime / Claudiodivizia p18 (UK), Dreamstime / Steve Allen p18 (Chile), Dreamstime / Fottoo p18 (Germany), Dreamstime / Denisismagilov p18 (Japan), Dreamstime / Odm p18 (Mexico), Dreamstime / Vicente Barcelo Varona p18 (Spain), Dreamstime / Delstudio p19(t), p19(1), Dreamstime / Byelikova p19(2), Dreamstime / Scaliger p19(3), Dreamstime / Sborisov p19(4), Dreamstime / Sean Pavone p19(5), Dreamstime / Ogonkova p19 (cappuccino), p19 (hamburger), Dreamstime / Lesssia p19 (movie ticket), Dreamstime / Tastyvector p19 (hotel), Dreamstime / Ye Liew p20(a), Dreamstime / Patrickmak039 p20(b), Dreamstime / Kamil Zablocki p20(c), Dreamstime / Georgii Dolgykh p20(d), Dreamstime / Elena Eryomenko p20(e), Dreamstime / Funandrejs p20(f), Dreamstime / Gerasimovvv p21(1), Dreamstime / Swinnerrr p21(2), Dreamstime / Jay Beiler p21(3), Dreamstime / Mykola Lukash p21(4), Dreamstime / Tifonimages p21(5), Dreamstime / Aleksandra Durdyn p21(6), Dreamstime / Steve Allen p21(7), Dreamstime / Tomas1111 p21(8), Dreamstime / Wavebreakmedia Ltd p25(t), Dreamstime / Lisa F. Young p25(b), Dreamstime / Marcin Kempski p26(a), Dreamstime / Laurin Rinder p26(b), Dreamstime / Leung Cho Pan p26(c), Dreamstime / Ashumskiy p26(d), Dreamstime / Jhernan124 p28(a), Dreamstime / Georgesheldon p28(c), Dreamstime / Kaspars Grinvalds p28(d), Dreamstime / Baoshengrulai p28(e), Dreamstime / Richard Thomas p28(f), Dreamstime / Pattilabelle p30(l), Dreamstime / Meinzahn p30(tr), Dreamstime / Abdurahman p30 (mr), Dreamstime / Viacheslav Iacobchuk p30(br), Dreamstime / Dmitrijs Dmitrijevs p31, Dreamstime / Sonulkaster p32(1), p32(2), p32(3), p32(4), p32(5), p32(6), p32(7), Dreamstime / Olivera Lozic p32(8), Dreamstime / Rpianoshow p33(ba), Dreamstime / Andrea De Martin p33(bb), Dreamstime / Nyul p33(bc), Dreamstime / Igor Mojzes p33(bd), Dreamstime / Ian Allenden p33(bf), Dreamstime / Gpointstudio p34(a), Dreamstime / Dmytro Zinkevych p34(b), Dreamstime / Eduard Bonnin Turina p34(c), Dreamstime / Alexey Sinelnikov p34(d), Dreamstime / Marcin Ciesielski / Sylwia Cisek p34(e), Dreamstime / Citalliance p34(f), Dreamstime / Stephen Coburn p34(g), Dreamstime / Iofoto p34(h), Dreamstime / Arne9001 p34(m), Dreamstime / Alla Leonova p35(t), Dreamstime / Tetsuobuseteru p35(bl), Dreamstime / Dean Bertoncelj p36(b), Dreamstime / Ominaesi p37(t1), Dreamstime / Kakigori p37(t2), Dreamstime / Andrei Krauchuk p37(t3), Dreamstime / Kakigori p37(t4), p37(t5), p37(t6), p37(t7), p37(t8 lawyer), p37(t9), p37(t10), p37(t11), p37(t12), p37(t13), p37(t15), Dreamstime /Aleksandr Popovskii p37 (t8 court house), Dreamstime / Ildar Galeev p37(t14), Dreamstime / Ideastud p37(b1), Dreamstime / Alancotton p37(b2), Dreamstime / Binkski p37(b3), Dreamstime / Vecstock Fee p37(b4), Dreamstime / Teichman p37(b4 clock), Dreamstime / Rasà Messina Francesca p37(b5), Dreamstime / Kannaa p37(b6), Dreamstime / Christian Muellerclausnitzer p37(b6 clock), Dreamstime / Meinzahn p38(1), Dreamstime / Julien Hautcoeur p38(2), Dreamstime / Bennymarty p38(3), Dreamstime / Paul Hakimata p38(4), Dreamstime / Dmitry Ilyshev p38(5), Dreamstime / Alexandre Fagundes De Fagundes p38(6), Dreamstime / Leungphotography p38(7), Dreamstime / Maxim Lupascu p39(a), Dreamstime / Aleksey Boldin p40(phone) p40 (phone), Dreamstime / Brett Critchley p40 (phone screen), Dreamstime / Daniel Kaesler p40(1), Dreamstime / Empada78 p40(2), Dreamstime / Emotionart p40(3), Dreamstime / David Melian p40(5), Dreamstime / Ilja Mašík p41, Dreamstime / Roman Tiraspolsky p42(ta), p42(tb), Dreamstime / Jimmy Lopes p42(tc), Dreamstime / Garn Phakathunya p42(td), Dreamstime / Andy Katz p42(bl), Dreamstime / Ryan Deberardinis p42(bm), Dreamstime / Kenneth Summers p42(br), Dreamstime / Christos Georghiou p43(1), Dreamstime / Bilha Golan p43(2), Dreamstime / Artisticco Llc p43(3), p43(4), Dreamstime / Kannaa p43(5), Dreamstime / Stanislav Ratushnyi p43(6), Dreamstime / Serhii Batazhuk p43(7), Dreamstime / Artisticco Llc p43(8), Dreamstime / Amateurphoto920 p43(9), Dreamstime / Artisticco Llc p43(10), p43(11), Dreamstime / Jpldesigns p43(12), Dreamstime / Dannyphoto80 p43(13), Dreamstime / Ginger Art p43(14), Dreamstime / Artisticco Llc p43(15), Dreamstime / Fashionstock .com p44(c), Dreamstime / Ruslan1117 p44(d), Dreamstime / Micro10x p46(al), Dreamstime / Robert Kneschke p46(ar), Dreamstime / Valuavitaly p46(bl), Dreamstime / Saša Prudkov p46(br), Dreamstime / Ian Allenden p46(cl), Dreamstime / Monkey Business Images p46(cr), Dreamstime / Mimagephotography p47(a), Dreamstime / Pojoslaw p47(b), Dreamstime / Mimagephotography p47(c), Dreamstime / Vladislav Lukyanov p47 (laundry), p47 (phone), p47 (piano), p47 (mail), Dreamstime / Frankmerfort p48(br), Dreamstime / Vadim Yerofeyev p49(t1), p49(t2), p49(t3), p49(t4), Dreamstime / Rtsubin p49(t5), Dreamstime / Natalia Zakharova p49(t6), Dreamstime / Nbvf p49(t7), Dreamstime / Roman Samokhin p49(t8), Dreamstime / Galina Drokina p49(t9), Dreamstime / RorygezFresh p49(t10), Dreamstime / Dule964 p49(t11), Dreamstime / Nuiiun p49(b1), Dreamstime / Yehor Vlasenko p49(b2), Dreamstime / Nuiiun p49(b3), p49(b4), p49(b5), p49(b6), p49(b7), p49(b9), p49(b10), p49(b11), p49(b12), p49(b13), p49(b14), Dreamstime / Ylivdesign p49(b8), p51 (jacket), Dreamstime / Ctrlaplus1 p50(t), Dreamstime / Benchart p51(bed), Dreamstime / Svetlana Yashina p51 (briefcase), Dreamstime / Dannyphoto80 p51 (food), Dreamstime / Mangsaab p51 (lock), Dreamstime / Nuiiun p51 (dress), p51 (shoes), p51 (skirt), Dreamstime / Hanohiki p51(1), Dreamstime / Ixuskmitl p51(2), Dreamstime / Mariusz Blach p51(3), Dreamstime / Juliengrondin p51(4), Dreamstime / Pranodh Mongkolthavorn p51(5), Dreamstime / Viorel Dudau p51(6), Dreamstime / Eq Roy p51(7), Dreamstime / Anibal Trejo p51(8), Dreamstime / Sborisov p51(9), Dreamstime / Christian Bertrand p52(m), Dreamstime / Prudencio Alvarez p52(bl), Dreamstime / Stockyimages p53(l), Dreamstime / Mariusz Prusaczyk p53(r), Dreamstime / Starstock p54(t1), p56(t1), Dreamstime / Sbukley p54(t2), p56(t2), Dreamstime / Featureflash p54(t3), p56(t3), Dreamstime / Starstock p54(t4), p56(t4), Dreamstime / Featureflash p54(t5), p56(t5), Dreamstime / Starstock p54(t6), p56(t6), Dreamstime / Featureflash p54(m1), p56(m1), Starstock / Dreamstime p54(m2), p56(m2), Dreamstime / Jenta Wong p54(m3), p56(m3), Dreamstime / Featureflash p54(m4), p56(m4), Dreamstime / Markwaters p54(m5), p56(m5), Dreamstime / Dimarik16 p54(b1), Dreamstime / Monkey Business Images p54(b2), Dreamstime / Noriko Cooper p54(b3), Dreamstime / Iakov Filimonov p55(ta), Dreamstime / Ekaterina Bykova p55(tb), Dreamstime / R. Gino Santa Maria / Shutterfree, Llc p55(tc), Dreamstime / Trak p55(m), Dreamstime / Ammentorp p55(ba), p57(ba), Dreamstime / Vadymvdrobot p55(bb), p57(bb), Dreamstime / Alex N p55(bc) p57(bc), Dreamstime / Citalliance p55(bd), p55(bd), Dreamstime / Steve Allen p56(ba), Dreamstime / Kenneth Sponsler p56(bb), Dreamstime / Monkey Business Images p56(bc), Dreamstime / Rocketclips, Inc. p57(ta), Dreamstime / Mcpics p57(tb), Dreamstime / Diego Vito Cervo p57(tc), Dreamstime / Madrugadaverde p57(m), Dreamstime / Ievgen Melamud p59 (a), Dreamstime / Pixxart p59 (b), Dreamstime / Scanrail p59 (c), Dreamstime / Michał Rojek p59 (d), Dreamstime / Danilo Sanino p59 (e); Dreamstime / Monkey Business Images p59(ba), Dreamstime / Dimarik16 p59(bb), Dreamstime / Dan Grytsku p59(bc), Dreamstime / Auremar p59(bd), Dreamstime / Wavebreakmedia Ltd p59(be), Dreamstime / Monkey Business Images p61(t), Dreamstime / Warrengoldswain p61(ml), Dreamstime / Liliya Bondarenko p61(mr), Dreamstime / Matimix p61(bl), Dreamstime / Nyul p61(br); Getty Images / Jan Hetfleisch p10(t), Getty / David M. Benett p10(b), Getty / Christie Goodwin p11(t), Getty / Jim McIsaac p11(O), Getty / Stefania D'Alessandro p16(bl), Getty / Clasos / CON p16(1), Getty / Marcelo Benitez / CON p16(3), Getty / David McNew p16(4), Getty / Graham Denholm p18(tl), Getty / Scott Olson p18(tm), Getty / Axelle/Bauer-Griffin p18(tr), Getty / Feng Li p18(bl), Getty / Bloomberg p18(bm), Getty / Dimitrios Kambouris p24(t), Getty / Bruce Glikas p24(b), Getty / Bloomberg p28(b), Getty / Tim Boyle p33(ta), Getty / Matt Cardy p33(tb), Getty / Raul Sifuentes p33(tc), Getty / Bloomberg p33(td), Getty / Nancy R. Schiff p33(te), Getty / Paul Natkin p33(tf), Getty / Bobby Bank p33(be), Getty / Dave Kotinsky p34(b), Getty / Timur Emek p39(b), Getty / Melodie Jeng p39(c), Getty / Alexander Spatari p40(4), Getty / Carlos Rodrigues p44(a), Getty / Koji Hirano p44(b), Getty / holgs p45(1), Getty / ferrantraite p45(2), Getty / VisitBritain/Ben Selway p45(3), Getty / JGI/Tom Grill p52(br), p52(t), Getty / Francis Specker / CBS p54(m6), p54(m6).

CANIEM No. 2275

Macmillan Publishers S.A. de C.V. Insurgentes Sur 1886
Col. Florida, CP 01030
Álvaro Obregón
Ciudad de México
Tel: +52 (55) 5482 2200
elt@grupomacmillan.com

www.grupomacmillan.com www.macmillan.com.mx www.macmillanenglish.com

These materials may contain links for third party websites.

We have no control over, and are not responsible for, the contents of such third party websites. Please use care when accessing them.

Printed in Brazil

This book was printed in September, 2017 by: Eskenazi Indústrica Gráfica Ltda, Avenida Miguel Frias Vasconcelos, 1023 - Jaguaré - São Paulo - SP.

Impresso no Brasil,EGB Editora Gráfica Bernardi Ltda,10 2024